The Framework of Our Faith

The Framework of Our Faith

Harold W. Burgess

Assurance Press

An imprint of:

Bristol House, Ltd.
Evangel Publishing House
Francis Asbury Society

Foreword

Framework of Our Faith is the result of a proposal made by sixteen Asbury Theological Seminary students to produce a readable statement of basic Wesleyan theology for laypersons seeking to find a structure for their faith. On their own initiative, these students committed themselves to writing this book, with the provision that I serve as the teacher of record for "Theological Thought for Instructional Settings." The late Dr. Louis E. Caister, then Academic Dean, enthusiastically endorsed the project and supported it with a significant investment of his own time.

The members of the class organized themselves into three groups with each group assuming the responsibility for writing four chapters. Thus chapters 2-5 became the responsibility of Ginny Wathen, Thane Ury, John Eshelman, and Roy Leddy with Vicki Walker as group leader. Chapters 6-9 were written by David Harrison, Carolyn Berg, Linda Goldston, Sam Bartlett and David Sears with Stan Tyson as group leader. Mary Lynne Peterson, Rindi Bowman, Linda Goldston, and Wayne Nichols with Margaret Dunn as group leader wrote chapters 10-13. Dean Caister wrote the introductory chapter.

This project from an "independent study" class in January 1983 remains one of my most treasured memories from thirty-seven years of teaching. Over the years I have received numerous requests to republish this useful little book. I have followed the advice of my friend, Joe Allison, an experienced editor: "Revise a little, but don't rewrite *Framework of Our Faith*. Its direct language communicates clearly and conveys an enthusiasm for the subject that must not be lost."

It will be obvious to some readers that the original writers of this book made considerable use of John Lawson's *Introduction to Christian Doctrine*. They did so with Dr. Lawson's blessing and encouragement. Indeed, he pronounced it a worthy theological text for England's lay pastors.

Harold W. Burgess
August 2005

Table of Contents

Chapter One

Getting Started

The intent of this book is to communicate the fundamentals of Christian theology (the framework) to the reader in an understandable way. After having considered the message of this small book, you should have a more satisfying grasp of the elements of our Christian faith and its message.

When you are introduced to a stranger for the first time, you realize that it is only the beginning of a new relationship. You learn the name, and a little about the individual. If you wish to get better acquainted with the person, you will need time to spend in conversation and fellowship. It takes a lifetime of such learning to get a deep understanding of the facets of the personality of one's true friend. Our hope is that this introduction to the fundamental beliefs of the Christian faith will whet your appetite to want to know more about God. We will suggest various resources along the way, most of them will be found in the Bible. It really should be at hand as you read this book.

The reader will observe that *The Framework of Our Faith* generally follows the Apostles' Creed. The creed is a short statement of basic doctrines recited in many congregations every Sunday. For many of us, it is all too easy to recite the creed without actually thinking about its content. This small book will enable the reader to have a better understanding of what one is saying when reciting the creed.

The Apostles' Creed has a long history. Its basic elements were used in the first Christian century as a brief statement of faith for those being baptized. In that context it seems to have been something of a checklist of beliefs for individuals being formally inducted into the fellowship of the church.

Our purpose in bringing this book to you is twofold: First, we seek to present the fundamental elements of the Christian faith in an understandable way. Secondly, its larger purpose is to encourage you, if you have not already done so, to make a personal faith commitment to our Lord and Savior, Jesus Christ.

Some individuals may hold back from making a personal faith commitment because it appears to be unreasonable. We acknowledge that a faith commitment requires one to go beyond reason, but we also affirm that one's faith commitment is reasonable. We hope, then, to provide a foundation for reasoning about and for understanding "The Faith." It is surely helpful to have some understanding in order to make a wholehearted "leap of faith" into a personal relationship with Jesus Christ.

In considering the matter of taking that step of faith, we face a basic problem. The problem is our desire for personal autonomy (freedom). "Mommy, I do it meself!" is the exclamation of a small child seeking to establish a sense of personal independence and freedom in the course of daily life. In the growing child, a developing sense of independence is essential to ultimate personal integrity and a proper sense of personal self-worth. In this struggle to be reborn into a right relationship with

God, we often want to claim control of our human destiny. In other words, to use an old-fashioned idiom, we want to hold the reins on our journey with God. Hence the attraction of the erroneous idea of "earning" our own salvation.

The whole point of the gospel message is that we are to live our lives intentionally by the righteousness and grace of God. God has, through His unmerited favor (grace), made the avenue of salvation available through trusting in what God has done for us, and not in what we are able to do for ourselves. The Apostle Paul, writing to the Galatian church, inquired of them, "Did you receive the Spirit by works of law, or by hearing with faith?" As the passage continues, Paul presses the Galatian Christians to consider whether their salvation had come through fulfilling the Jewish (religious) law or by faith (3:2-5). In our daily lives we need to consider seriously the same issue—does our salvation come through successfully leaping over religious hurdles or does it come through our faith lived out in action?

In these pages we want to encourage you either individually, or as a class, to discuss the various points of emphasis. We encourage you to turn to your Bible and examine the particular Scripture references given and the context of them. It will also be helpful for you to consult a Bible dictionary, to examine an available commentary on the Bible, or to read some of the recent paraphrases of Scripture in your search for comprehension. Each or all of these suggested aids to study can open new windows of understanding. In this process you are following the footsteps of those who have gone before. Every one of us has had to struggle with the meaning of Scripture and its implications for our daily lives. One hopes that you will experience that flash of insight, the "ah ha" experience, when suddenly that which has been vague, misunderstood, or unclear comes into clear focus. It is at this point of understanding that we are most dependent upon the Holy Spirit. In the midst of our confusion and search, He is the One who is our Teacher and Illuminator

(John 14:26).

As part of our heritage, we have received an approach to understanding and belief that incorporates four elements: Scripture, tradition, reason, and experience. The Scriptures are the cornerstone and foundation of our beliefs. Those beliefs are then examined in the light of the long tradition of the Christian Church and the exercise of reason. The final step is the application of experience. Each of these elements has been included in our efforts to state our beliefs and to communicate with you.

We invite the reader to join us in these pages to consider the common agreements regarding our faith; and then to join us as we seek to flesh out the meaning of the brief creedal statements. We hope that the following chapters will provide a reasonable foundation for your growing faith.

Creedal affirmations alone are not the same as saving faith. So as we study the Bible in conjunction with this book, we will remember that:

The Bible is more than a volume of hitherto unknown facts about God, man and the universe. It is a book of exhortation based upon those facts. By far the greater portion of the book is devoted to an urgent effort to persuade people to alter their ways and bring their lives into harmony with the will of God as set forth in its pages . . . Theological truth is useless until it is obeyed. The purpose behind all doctrine is to secure moral action. A. W. Tozer, *Renewed Day by Day* (Grand Rapids: Baker, 1980), 16.

Chapter Two

Belief in God

"I believe in God the father Almighty"
(The Creed)

I. I Believe

When we think of the word faith we usually define it as a personal belief and trust in the love and power of God. Faith's foundation lies in the realization that God is Truth (John 14:6). Our faith is based upon certain facts and truths, but these do not stand alone since the acknowledgement of facts alone will not make a believer out of anyone. We must have a personal faith that affects our lives and the lives of others.

The word faith has two common uses that should be distinguished. First: "The Faith" includes all biblically based knowledge such as teachings about God, Christ, the Holy Spirit, man's relationship with God, and salvation. This is "the Faith," as in Galatians 1:23; Ephesians 4:5; and Jude 3. A further example of this first use is seen in a familiar hymn:

Faith of our fathers! living still
In spite of dungeon, fire, and sword,
O how our hearts beat high with joy
When e'er we hear that glorious word!
Faith of our fathers, holy faith!
We will be true to thee till death.

The second use of faith describes the personal experience of believing or knowing the truth of "the Faith." This experience may be described as an encounter with God resulting in a loving, personal trust in Him and in Jesus Christ as His Son and our Savior. Such faith may be referred to as "Christian saving faith." An experience of this type of faith is illustrated in the hymn:

My faith looks up to Thee,
Thou Lamb of Calvary,
Savior divine!
Now hear me while I pray,
Take all my guilt away,
O let me from this day
Be wholly Thine!

Faith involves both the head and the heart. Though faith is certainly a part of the intellect and is a matter of the will, it becomes more real when it is a part of experience. When faith is put into action through total trust in God, then no matter what the circumstances faith will grow. The writer of Hebrews explains it this way, "Now faith is the assurance of things hoped for, the conviction of things not seen" (11:1).

When we have an experience with God, we naturally begin to form a structure of beliefs. In other words, through critical examination and reflection, we will come to certain logical conclusions that form the framework for our faith. Whether we use the term or not, this is our theology. To put it very simply, theology is what we believe about God and our relationship to Him.

Two Aspects of Religious Authority

We find two chief aspects of religious authority. First, our faith rests on the authority of the Bible. It is the only record of facts concerning Christ such as Old Testament prophecies and the Gospel accounts of His birth, life, ministry, message, death and resurrection. Because our faith rests in Jesus Christ as our Savior, we believe that every true Christian doctrine must be in accord with Scripture. Therefore, a fundamental understanding of Scripture is critical in forming our own theology. We will then have a firm basis for our faith. We can give reliable guidance to others in their understanding of facts recorded in the Bible (cf. chapter 11 of this book).

Secondly, our authority comes from the immediate work of the Holy Spirit in our hearts and lives. Beyond the plain facts of Scripture, we become aware of a sense of "rightness" concerning our faith in God. This is confirmed by the Holy Spirit's presence in our hearts, and through such means as fellowship, prayer, and the fruit of the Spirit (Gal. 5:22, 23). The Holy Spirit is our comforter and teacher. Jesus said that He would come to "teach you all things, and bring to your remembrance all that I have said to you" (John 14:26). Thus the Holy Spirit works through the Scriptures, but also directly in the hearts of people (cf. chaps. 8 and 11 of this book).

Although some people fear that in describing God we limit Him and bring Him down to human terms, everyone has some concept of God. Though the nature of God is complex and often difficult to understand (Rom. 11:33, 34; Isa. 55:8-9), He has chosen to make His characteristics known to us, chiefly through the life of His only Son Jesus Christ.

II. Attributes of God

First, God is <u>transcendent</u>. This means that although God created the universe and all that exists, He is not confined to the limits of space and time, as we understand them. In other words, God exists in His own right, apart from His creation. He is without beginning and without end (Rev. 22:13).

Second, God is <u>immanent</u>. Although He exists apart from His creation, He has direct contact with it. As Christians we believe that God is in sovereign control of everything that exists. The physical and natural laws, which govern us, are an expression of His control.

Third, God is a <u>personal</u> living God (Deut. 5:26; Jer. 10:10; Acts 14:15). He is more than a "force." God thinks, feels, and responds to His creation. He has personal contact with the world, and seeks fellowship with people. He is interested in each of us (I Pet. 5:7) and has <u>made provision</u> for us to have a personal <u>relationship with Him</u> through His son Jesus Christ. (John 14:23). Therefore, our worship should be a joyous celebration of His relationship with us. True Christian worship, accordingly, is much more than an abstract meditation about a far-away God.

One way God is known to us is as "<u>our Father</u>." A father disciplines, loves, forgives, and encourages his child. God maintains these same characteristics in His relationship to us, and it is a privilege that we can call Him "Abba, Father." (Rom. 8:15).

In studying the Christian faith, it is well to be aware of the <u>drawbacks</u> we have in communicating about spiritual and metaphysical matters. We are studying a God whose properties and practices are supernatural. In our inadequate human terms, we use words such as father to explain our understanding of God. However, this can cause problems, because <u>we all have our perceptions and past experiences</u>. For example, a girl whose father has abused her will likely have difficulty in responding positively to a God who is like a father. Though such comparisons will never be entirely adequate, they can give us a toehold for under-standing God's ways with His creation.

As expressed in the Apostles' Creed, God is the Father Almighty, the sovereign ruler of all things, and the source of all power. This does not mean that God causes all things to happen. God created us with minds of our own. He granted us the free-dom to choose. This accounts for many problems in our world today that are not the result of God's will. He permits some sit-uations because He allows us to make our own choices. However, He can use any situation in life that is yielded to Him and work in it for good (Rom. 8:28).

Given to us are two basic alternatives concerning the exis-tence of God: He either exists or He does not exist. Our basic assumption here affects how we view the universe. A person who does not believe that God exists generally sees the universe as random and irrational. The materialist assumes that nothing exists beyond the physical universe. Such a one seeks at best to discover and understand the physical world. This viewpoint may lead to seeing life as pointless and in turn may lead to despair.

Christians believe that God exists. Thus, we perceive the universe as basically orderly and that we are a part of a sys-tematic, rational universe. This orderliness is reflected in the pattern of the changing seasons and in the orbiting of the planets around the sun. An orderly creation allows humankind, through the scientific method, to discover and to understand much about our world. The methods of science are not sufficient to discover all of God. However, He does partially disclose Himself to us through natural revelation. As Christians, then, we believe that objects exist and that events occur with a purpose.

Human beings are the climax of creation. We are self-con-scious, thinking, feeling, and capable of making intellectual and moral choices. We are spiritual as well as physical beings. Our spiritual natures are separate from our physical bodies although they work in and through the confines of our physical bodies. The source of all is a Personal Being, a living God who is not merely a law of existence. He is a spiritual being, not having a physical body, and He is not confined to time and space.

The Creator of humankind embodies rich and complex characteristics at least partially shared with His creation. Not only is He infinite and perfect, He is also personal and loving. He is the sovereign ruler of the universe, but He chooses to dwell in our hearts and to express Himself to us within our frame of understanding. I Corinthians 3:16 sums it up well: "Do you not know that you are God's temple and that God's Spirit dwells in you?" With similar import, the writer of Acts quotes Paul as saying, "In him we live and move and have our being" (17:28).

Yet because of our finiteness, we can never completely understand everything about God. God does not drive either the skeptic or the unbeliever into a corner with facts that may not be challenged. This guarantees that our faith in and love for God shall be free. There will often be some question or gap in information that calls for a step of faith on the part of each of us.

Chapter Three

God the Creator

[I believe in God the Father Almighty,] "Maker of Heaven and Earth"
(The Creed)

I. Revelation and Inspiration

Revelation is a term used to designate the process by which God reveals Himself to humankind. It also refers to the truth that He has revealed. Essential in these meanings is the recognition that a person's knowledge of God is the result of God's decision to make Himself known. Because God is infinite and holy and because humanity is finite and sinful, we know nothing about God that He has not first revealed to us through His love and goodness (Job 32:8).

Revelation is commonly classified as either general revelation or special revelation. General revelation is the divine truth made known to all people through nature. This is knowledge God gives us about Himself apart from the Scriptures (Rom. 1:19-20). David expresses this kind of general revelation in

Psalm 19:1 where we read, "The heavens are telling the glory of God; and the firmament proclaims his handiwork."

Special revelation refers to the revelation of God that we have received in the Bible and in the person of Christ. Through the Bible we learn truths that are not evident in nature, such as the Incarnation, the Trinity, and the Atonement. The Personal disclosure of God in His Son Jesus Christ is the most important example of special revelation.

Besides the direct and indirect revealing of God's truths to humanity, God also inspires us. The word *inspiration* implies acknowledgment of God's supernatural influence in the lives of His people through the activity of the Holy Spirit. This influence comes by way of revelation from the Holy Spirit who makes possible our understanding of what God has revealed. See I Corinthians 2, especially verses 12-13. Such knowledge does not imply a suspension of natural human abilities, since God's gifts make one fully human. As Christians, we recognize the Bible as the greatest and most important work of revelation and inspiration (II Tim. 3:16). The Holy Spirit is still active today in guiding us to understand God's revelation.

II. Maker of Heaven and Earth

The word *creation* carries one basic meaning. We should not take lightly the fact that God caused to exist what did not exist and that His will is an adequate reason for whatever exists (Gen. 1:1; Ps. 33:6; Rev. 4:11). The Genesis record reads, "God said, 'Let there be . . . and it was so. . . .'" All was created from nothing by His word since there was no preexisting matter. At the end of time, as we know it, we are told in II Peter 3:10 that, ". . . the heavens will pass away with a loud noise, and the elements will be dissolved with fire, and the earth and the works that are upon it will be burned up." Therefore, the created universe, unlike God, has both beginning and ending (Ps. 90:2; Isa. 51:6;

Rev. 20:11). God who is complete within Himself created the universe out of His love.

One goal of Christian thought has been to begin to grasp the meaning of God's sovereignty. The concept of God as Creator, as Governor, and as Preserver signifies that the universe is not meaningless. There is a purpose for creation and in this purpose is the answer to the question as to why the Creation took place.

The long-standing debate between individuals who call themselves creationists and those who call themselves evolutionists has become a divisive force between Christians. It is the unanimous conclusion of the writers of this book that there are sufficient grounds for us to agree that God is the Creator and that His will is sufficient cause for creation of the universe. Opinions as to exactly how He did it, and the length of time involved, need not obscure our belief in His ultimate purpose.

Through His creation, God has revealed Himself to be consistent through His actions. We see this in the continuity of nature, also known as natural law. Natural law is important to Christian belief, for it gives us confidence that our lives follow an orderly plan and that God is in control.

Some materialistic naturalists have challenged the belief that God governs nature and its laws. Tension between a naturalistic view of the world and the Christian view is one that cannot be easily resolved. We view the world as under the sovereign control of God, but some naturalistic scientists observing the same data deny the concept of an immanent God. If the world is governed only by predictable natural laws, as the naturalist says, there can be no caring God who answers prayer and breaks into the earthly order of things. Christians view the predictability of natural laws as evidence of God's love and care.

The orderliness of the universe argues for the existence of a creator. If one agrees at this point, then it is not hard to acknowledge that the creator could not be a prisoner of his own creation. Thus, we recognize that God is able to work within His natural laws to cause things to happen in ways beyond normal expectations. Such events are not necessarily in contradiction to natural laws. They give evidence of God operating in a sphere, which is superior to, yet coexistent with, natural law.

We understand our God as One who speaks to us, fellowships with us, answers our prayers, and cares for our needs in ways that the world cannot explain. There is some mystery in God's ways and means. He does not always answer our prayers as we desire. He does not always guide us in the direction we would choose to go. Yet experience proves that He does answer, guide and bless us. God can be expected to answer prayer and to care for His children with resources that are beyond mere human understanding. We refer to such workings as "divine Providence."

III. Miracles

A miracle is an extraordinary event that is beyond our power to do or to understand, God is always the source of such events. The idea of a God who works primarily on the level of the supernatural is an idea with roots in Greek thought rather than the Bible. In Hebrew thinking, little distinguishes the natural from the supernatural. God is the direct or indirect cause of every single event, from falling rain to the parting of the Red Sea. In a thought system where every event is considered an act of God, every event has an element of miracle. Thus it is hardly possible for the Hebrew mind to think in terms of a religious life without the reality of *miracle*.

While miracles are sometimes described as a "suspension" of the natural order, such is not always the case. The fact that we can not understand how an event occurs does not affect the process by which it happens. Some miracles may simply be instances of God working through natural laws that may not yet be known to us.

Biblical miracles served as heralds of the Messianic age (Matt. 11:4-5; Luke 7:22) and were designed to stir the people to belief and repentance (Matt. 11:20-21; Luke 10:13). Miracles always had a purpose. At least sixteen times in the Pentateuch (the first five books of the Bible) it is evident that the purpose of miracles was to cause all men to know that God is the only true and living God. It seems clear that God has at many times and places performed miracles to prove that He is the living God. The experience of the Church strongly suggests that miracles typically occur at times of spiritual crises.

The resurrection of Jesus Christ is the supreme miracle recorded in the Bible. It turned the Crucifixion into a tremendous triumph over evil and death. Biblical miracles are convincing. But as *fresh* evidences of God's *present* activity are perceived our faith is given a living quality. God still uses miracles today in situations and with people as He sees fit. He, however, is never a mere showman. His miracles are meant to minister and to open doubting hearts and minds.

IV. The Supernatural

A substantial number of us find it difficult to comprehend the supernatural, the idea that God is able by His power to overrule the natural order of His providential government of the world. It will be helpful to look at it from two different perspectives.

First, there is the aspect of scientific discovery. Current advances in science have achieved today what would have been considered miracles only a few years ago. If we achieve today what yesterday's knowledge could not imagine, how can we say that the infinite mind of God cannot perform the miraculous? Obviously we cannot. In fact, we must go so far as to admit that no matter how wide the knowledge of humanity expands, God's ways will be infinitely higher, and His workings will be beyond our comprehension (Isa. 55:8-11).

Second, it seems obvious that modes of describing an event were considerably different in the past than they are now. If modern people were to go back in time they would describe an event quite differently from that of an earlier time. The reason is that they would be drawing from an entirely different frame of reference. This in no way discounts the element of the miraculous. Further, it is well to remember that each age has its skeptics; biblical times were not exempt.

Christian thought has traditionally affirmed that God's creation includes all things "visible and invisible." The physical universe of matter and force, which is observed, is not all that exists. Other created beings exist. They do not possess material bodies like ours, yet they have form and are capable of feeling, thinking, speaking, listening and having a sense of moral responsibility. Angels have been created by God and reflect His spiritual image. They are, among other terms, referred to as celestial beings, spirits, the sons of God, dwellers in heaven, the host of heaven, the army of the Lord, and the spirits that minister before the throne of God.

Most Christians have had no direct experience with angels. However, we believe in angels because the Bible affirms that they exist. The Scriptures depict God as being attended by a host of angels who serve as messengers between God and man. Sometimes they reveal God's intentions and sometimes they act as intercessors for humanity.

The Bible uses the term angel to translate the Greek and Hebrew words for *messenger*. These terms commonly refer to an order of supernatural or heavenly beings who act as God's messengers. These beings are also seen in other roles. There are instances of angels contending with Satan and providing unseen aid on our behalf (Dan. 6:22; 10:10-14; II Kings 6:15-17). The Bible clearly teaches that God has countless angels at His command. The unseen world of angels cannot be described adequately because it has not been fully disclosed to us. Scripture does not give much detail about angels, but it does say they will be a source of might and comfort in all circumstances for us. (Psa. 91:11-12).

Chapter Four

The Jesus of History

[I believe in] "Jesus Christ, His Only Son, Our Lord"
(The Creed)

I. Historical Religion

One essential characteristic of the Christian faith is that it is not a construction of the human mind. Nor is it only an ethical system or a philosophy. Rather, our faith is an intellectual and heart-felt agreement with the historical facts of the faith. The extent to which the Christian faith is established on historical fact is sometimes debated among individuals holding to either traditional or critical opinions regarding the nature of the Church.

Certain skeptics doubt the truth of the biblical account of the Incarnation, life, death, and resurrection of Christ. Some critical theologians have gone to great lengths in attempting to offer what they believe is a more plausible interpretation of what the Bible says. As a result, some have been led to doubt the accuracy of the Bible. It is our position that every such attempt has detracted from the beauty of the truth set forth in the Scriptures.

When we consider what we know about God, we recognize that this knowledge is not only an idea created by the human mind. Rather, God revealed Himself to us in His Son, Jesus Christ, who came from heaven in human form. We further believe that there is more than enough historical documentation to provide satisfactory evidence that Jesus did live on earth. Christianity is an authoritative witness to the saving acts of God performed in the course of history. The focus of our faith is on the person, Jesus Christ.

Granted, all religions have some elements of truth; most religions have some meaningful code of ethics; indeed, some believe in "greater beings." Of course God reveals something of Himself through nature, but without a focus on the Jesus of history there is little distinction between Christianity and other religions. The Christian faith is about faith in God as He has revealed Himself to us through Jesus Christ.

Christianity is the religion of the Incarnation. The Creator of the world united Himself to His handiwork through the person of Jesus Christ. He was not a distant life that had no connection with reality as we know it. God came to us in our situation and condition and "dwelt among us." God united Himself with the world through His Son. Because of the obvious importance of Jesus' life and ministry, it is imperative that what Scripture says about Him be accepted as accurate, historical truth.

Mere knowledge of historical events concerning Jesus makes no one a Christian any more than knowledge about Kitty Hawk and the Wright Brothers makes one a pilot. Salvation comes to us by the moving of the mind, will, and affection so as to enable us to place our loving trust in Christ and offer our obedience to Him. Through believing in Jesus and yielding our lives to Him, we receive the salvation that God promised. Salvation is a personal response to that which God has actually done for humanity in His Son. We are saved by faith that comes through hearing the Word of God (Rom. 10:17). To summarize, Christian tradition affirms that the Bible is a reliable account of the historical events that relate to Jesus' life, death, and resurrection.

It is true that some reinterpret the Gospels in the light of modern information and scholarship. They base their reinterpretation on a view that the New Testament was written in terms that were meaningful to early Christians but are less than adequate for today's educated person. Some critics question the validity of the Gospels by stating that they are carefully arranged and edited accounts of certain ideas held by the early Church. According to these critics, what the Bible contains is not a true biography of the "Jesus of history," but is the Church's concept and understanding of Christ.

The goal of the Gospels was not simply to give a biography of Jesus' life. The authors wrote with the explicit goal of winning converts. Of course the Gospels are a historical record as well. They are accepted as reliable and as an accurate account of Jesus' character, teaching, death, and resurrection. In Scripture, and especially the Gospels, we are given sufficient basis for the historical faith.

II. Jesus Christ His only Son Our Lord

The development of our Christian faith can be traced from the fellowship of the disciples. The process can be seen in some of the New Testament titles for Jesus, as expressed in the Apostles' Creed. Jesus is the name given to our Lord at birth (Luke 2:21). It speaks of Him as a man among men. The name *Jesus* is derived from the Old Testament name *Joshua*, and means *savior*. His mother was instructed to give Him this name before His birth (Luke 1:31). Since Jesus was a common name, there were others with the same name (Col. 4:11).

A number of people recognized Jesus as a prophet because He was a man of commanding personality with an unparalleled grasp of spiritual things. He reminded those who knew Him of Old Testament prophets. His ability to teach and power to heal and cast out demons supported the prophet image (John 4:19; Matt. 16:13-14; Mark 6:15; Luke 7:16). At the beginning of His public ministry He was baptized by John in the Jordan River and received the baptism of the Holy Spirit, giving supernatural evidence of His deity (Mark 1:9-11). Jesus did not become the God Man with His baptism. He shared the very nature of God from the beginning. He was *incarnate* from the moment of His conception.

The title Christ is equivalent to the Hebrew word *Messiah*. Both words mean *the Anointed One*. The Jewish people's faith looked forward to the coming of Messiah. They expected Him to fulfill the prophecies and to rescue them from the bondage of their earthly oppression. Numerous Israelites in the time of Christ were expecting a kingly person to descend from heaven, to vanquish all foes, and to restore His kingdom.

Only a few people realized that restoration of His people was to be a restoration to holiness and obedience to God. These few knew that He would be from the family line of David (Isa. 9:7; I Chron. 17: 9-14; II Chron. 6:16) but they did not know what to expect. They did know they were the "chosen" people and they believed that He would reign over all peoples and bring divine blessings to all nations (Mic. 4:1-4). When people realized and proclaimed that Jesus was the Messiah, the faith increased. Through the revelation of God (Matt. 16:17) the accuracy of their earlier expectations and conceptions became more acute. This led, in turn, to their profession of Jesus as the Christ, the foundation upon which the Church is built (Matt. 16:18-19).

III. Names of Jesus

The name <u>*Son of Man*</u> finds its roots in the prophecy of Daniel (7:13) which presents the idea of the coming of "a son of man," implying God's coming world kingdom. This name is significant because it is <u>the name by which Jesus most frequently called Himself</u> (Matt. 16:13; Mark 2:10). He did not conceive of His role of king in terms of the world's understanding of *king*. Rather, <u>He saw Himself as a servant</u>, as one who gave and gave until He ultimately would give His life. By using this lowly title for Himself, Jesus acknowledged His personal pain, suffering, humility, and betrayal (Mark 10:45).

In the Old Testament, the kingdom of God is the sovereign power of God whereby He rules the world (Psa. 145:11-13). In the New Testament, the kingdom is the action of God and the gift of God (Luke 4:43). Though there is some difference of opinion as to the exact time of this kingdom, we must remember that <u>Jesus taught</u> that <u>the kingdom is both present and future</u>. It was certainly active and alive in His life and it was destined to continue to spread throughout the earth.

<u>The Church is the instrument of the kingdom</u>, though not the kingdom itself. Jesus taught that <u>the kingdom</u> was something that we could <u>enter into</u> and <u>actually be a part of</u> (Matt. 11:11; 7:21; 21:31; Mark 9:47; 10: 14-15; Luke 16:16; 22: 29-30). Jesus also spoke of "keys" to heaven. Some reason that perhaps the Church is a key or instrument for entering the kingdom.

The use of the term *Lord* in referring to Christ was a significant step for the early church. <u>By acknowledging Him as *Lord*</u>, Christians <u>made a significant personal commitment</u>. It indicated that they understood themselves as His subjects and subjects also of the gospel that He preached. Christians began to use the term *Lord* because they recognized that Jesus was doing what only God could do. Obedience to Him was important because they believed Him to be their Master, the very One on whom they must rest for salvation. Their attitude toward Christ was the same as one would properly have toward God.

Paul knew that pagans used the word *Lord* to refer to their cultic gods for salvation and he found it necessary to make a distinction. In I Corinthians 8:5-6 he notes that there are many gods, but supremely there is only one God and one Lord through whom and by whom we exist.

In the Old Testament we see that God is referred to as *Lord*. Likewise, in the New Testament we find the same term applied to Jesus, thus equating Him with God. The use of the expression *Lord* marked an extraordinary leap of faith in the early church. It expressed an acknowledgment that Jesus had done for them what only God could do. The members of the early church clearly recognized Jesus as equal with God and they trusted Him for salvation. While the first primitive confession that united the church was "Thou art the Christ" (Matt. 16:16), the characteristic creedal confession of the New Testament Church was "Jesus is Lord" (Phil. 2:11).

In acknowledging that Jesus is Lord, His deity is already recognized. However, the use of the title *Divine Son* made the developing doctrine of His divinity even more explicit. Jesus was understood as equal with God. The term *Divine* confirmed the Church's faith in this equality; the term *Son* provided the rationale for this conviction. A son and father are of "one flesh and blood," which is applied symbolically to Christ. Therefore, the idea of Jesus being the Divine Son conveys the idea of equality of divine status with God the Father (Matt.11:25-27; Luke 20: 9-13; John 1:18, 3:16; Acts 9:20; Heb.1:1-2; I John 4:10).

The Greek word *logos* has a wide variety of meanings, though it is perhaps most often translated as *word*. In John's Gospel this term is used to express profound truth almost as a play on words. Jesus is identified as *The Word*, present with God in the beginning and also being God in the beginning (John 1:1-

2). Just as the Genesis account of creation tells of God speaking the word and the creation coming forth, John places Jesus in the creation event as being synonymous with the word spoken by God; thus Christ is the agent of Creation (John 1:3).

Another meaning of *logos* is "reason." Christ is the reason (or logic) behind the Creation. Christ was God's Word in the literal sense that He was God's supreme communication to man. The concept of Christ as "the Word of God" provides a connection between the special revelation in Christ with the general revelation in intellectual and artistic activities of humanity. Jesus is the cause of "all things" and is seen as both the effective agent of creation (John 1:3) and also of restitution and judgment (Rev. 19:11-16).

Chapter Five

Jesus: God Incarnate

[I believe in Jesus Christ, His Only Son, Our Lord;]
"Who was conceived by the Holy Spirit [and] born of the Virgin Mary"
(The Creed)

I. The Incarnation

The Incarnation is the center of Christian belief. Without it Christianity would be meaningless, without purpose. The word *Incarnation* comes from the Latin word *carnis*, meaning "flesh." Many find this a difficult doctrine to understand, hence the exercise of one's faith is important. As reported in John 1:14, "the Word [Son of God] became flesh and dwelt among us." God united Himself to humanity through His divine Son, so that God became flesh, fully human yet fully divine. The Apostle Paul expresses the Incarnation as follows:

Christ Jesus, who, though he was in the form of God, did not count equality with God a thing to be grasped, but emptied himself, taking the form of a servant, being born in the likeness of men. And being found in human form, he humbled himself

and became obedient unto death, even death on a cross"
(Phil.2:5-8).

While in the flesh, Christ experienced the same limitations
of time and space that all persons experience. At the same time,
however, He had access to the divine powers that exceeded these
boundaries of time and space through His baptism and the
comming of The Spirit.

To help one understand how this can be, an analogy may be
helpful. Let us draw the analogy from present missionaries serving in a foreign land, where they live and work among the
nationals and adopt much of the local lifestyle. By living as the
nationals, such missionaries may gain acceptance and credibili-
ty with the local population. However, the missionaries do not
lose their citizenship nor do they lose their knowledge and
appreciation of their homeland and its familiar style of life.

To further the early church's understanding of the nature of
Christ, the doctrine of *kenosis* or "emptying" was advanced.
Kenosis suggests that Christ emptied Himself of all the divine
privileges except the characteristic of Divine love, which He
imparted to every believer. This is the love that God expressed
in Christ when He chose to take upon Himself the limitation of
humanity. God through Christ then expressed this love when He
chose to take upon Himself the limitations of humanity. Thus,
because of His self-imposed limitations, or abasement, God
could save humanity itself. Christ chose to become fully human
in order that we could be saved. At the same time, He did not
give up His deity by becoming man, for He was both fully
human and fully God (Phil 2:5-11; John 10:17-18).

There are several schools of thought about Jesus'
Incarnation. They range from believing that Jesus was only a
good man whom the Spirit inspired, to the position that Jesus
was completely God with only the appearance of being human.
In order to accept the Incarnation as truth, we believe that
Christ was both truly and properly human: that though He

remained the Son of God, He was also the Son of man. Because of this, He could make an offering of Himself for the atonement of our sins. If Christianity is to retain its character as a religion of divine redemption, the Incarnation is essential.

In order for any idea of salvation to be credible, we must affirm two things about our Lord. First, He must be fully divine. Second, He must be fully human. If He was not divine, then His life, death, and resurrection did not complete God's saving action in the world. If He was not human and did not go through the same temptations and struggles we face, then His saving action would not be where the problem is, within the realm of our human affairs, and we have no ground for any relationship with Him.

II. "Conceived by the Holy Spirit, born of the Virgin Mary"

As recorded in the Bible (Isa. 7:14; Matt. 1:18-23; Luke 1:26-31) and professed in the Creed, we believe that Christ was supernaturally conceived by an act of the Holy Spirit. Luke 1:34-35 states:

And Mary said to the angel, "How can this be, since I have no husband?" And the angel said to her, "The Holy Spirit will come upon you, and the power of the Most High will overshadow you; therefore the child to be born will be called holy, the Son of God."

This passage accounts for Jesus' divinity and humanity being combined in one physical body. From His mother He took His full humanity, and from God the Father, Christ took His full divinity. The conception itself is seen as an example of God's miraculous intervention in human history.

From the beginning, Christians have believed that Christ was conceived in the womb of the Virgin Mary. This was the work of the Holy Spirit without the physical act of intercourse. Thus, Christ received His humanity from a real human being.

Jesus spoke of Himself as "a man" (John 8:40), yet in one way He was different from everyone. He was the product of a union between God and God's own creation. It was divinely intended that He would be truly human, albeit without the sinful heritage of man. The Virgin Birth provides the desperately needed break from the natural law of cause/effect that carries forward the sinful heritage of the race.

God's love for humanity is demonstrated in the incarnation of Christ. In taking on human form, Christ knew He was subjecting Himself to suffering and humiliation. When one considers that the glory of the Father is beyond anything we could dream of, it is amazing that Christ chose to live as a man and to suffer and die for our sins. The fact that He did it overshadows any question of how He did it.

By the Incarnation, God chose to utilize the laws of human nature and not to suspend them. In other words, He did not have Jesus miraculously appear in Bethlehem. Instead, Jesus came in the conventional way in His physical birth. By choosing to cooperate, Mary was willing to be obedient to God's plan (Luke 1:38). Her complete trust and faith in God is a great example for all of us. Because of the Virgin Mary's obedience, she was chosen as the instrument for God's mightiest act, the Incarnation itself.

III. About Mary

Because of Mary's unique role in the Incarnation, many refer to her as the "Blessed Virgin Mary." This title is in accordance with Luke 1:48, which states, "For he has regarded the low estate of His handmaiden. For behold, henceforth all generations will call me blessed." What greater honor could a woman have than to be the mother of God Incarnate? What title is thus more fitting than "blessed"? However, Protestants traditionally reserve their adoration and praise for Christ, rather than His mother. Christ's attitude regarding adoration directed toward His mother can be seen in Luke 11:27-28. Elizabeth also recognized Mary as "the mother of my Lord" (Luke 1:43).

Generally, Protestants acknowledge the special position held by Mary in regard to the birth of Christ. At the same time, we place great emphasis on the fact that only God is to be worshiped. While Roman Catholic theologians may argue that the reverence accorded to Mary is on a different level than the worship of God, the differences are not readily apparent to the average Protestant. Because the Roman Catholic Church holds these ideas as official teachings, agreement between Protestants and Catholics is very difficult.

Chapter Six

The Word of the Cross

[I believe that He] "suffered under Pontius Pilate,
was crucified, dead, and buried;"
(The Creed)

I. The Suffering Christ

The prophet Isaiah states: <u>Surely he has borne our griefs</u> <u>and carried our sorrows</u>, yet we esteemed him stricken, smitten by God, and afflicted. But he was <u>wounded</u> for our transgressions, he was <u>bruised</u> for our iniquities (Isa. 53:4-5a).

II. The Mystery of Evil

An understanding of a suffering Savior first requires an awareness of <u>the need of a Savior</u>. Only after we have recognized what we are can we clearly see the splendor of what our Savior has done for us. "Evil" includes everything in life that is inconsistent with the good and wise plan of God. If we did not view the essential nature of God as love, evil would simply be a fact of life, not a mystery with which to struggle.

Evil may be partially defined as the suffering that exists as the result of man's fall. It includes all aspects of human suffering. Evil also includes rebellion against the moral and spiritual order of God. Rebellion is commonly called sin. In fact, most human suffering is a clue to the nature of sin. The effects of sin are clearly seen, for example, in the grief and pain that come from war, social injustice, family upheaval, even disease. Sin also makes death a fearful experience. The fact that we have locks, not just doors, and policemen, not just laws, is a common reminder of the impact of sin.

There is much discussion about what is meant by "sin." The "moral view" is the "common-sense" view from which society takes its laws. In this view, sin is an action for which one is morally accountable. One is held accountable because the person chose to break an accepted standard of the community. According to the moral view, sin is usually seen as trespassing society's law instead of God's law.

The "religious view" of sin seeks to answer the "whys" of life. Thus, the religious definition of sin is concerned not only with breaking the law, but also with the reason why an individual sins and with the results of one's behavior. Scripture teaches us that man sins because he is sinful by nature. In the presence of God's holiness, then, it is understandable that human beings often realize a sense of separation from God (Psa. 51:1-5, 10-12).

The first act of sin is seen in the opening chapters of the Bible. The Genesis story has some similarity to the folklore of other ancient cultures. These narratives or "tell-me-why stories" were told to answer the curiosity of questioning minds that found themselves in a mysterious world. They gave an answer to questions like, "Why are men ashamed when caught naked?" "Why is childbirth painful?" and so forth.

However, Genesis is not simply a story. It contains deep spiritual truth. Some might use the term "true truth." It is different and superior in content to folklore. No other "Book of Beginnings" presents such a deep understanding of the human heart. Its statements about Almighty God are also unique.

As the Genesis story unfolds we read that mankind was created in God's image and had the ability to fellowship with Him (1:26-27). Problems surfaced, however, when man sought to go beyond the God-given boundaries (3:1-6). The spiritual result was shame when found in the presence of the Creator (3:7-10). This "fall" from God's original setting was the beginning of humankind's separation from God and the entrance of shame, pain, expulsion, and death.

Another result of the Fall is that man's will is corrupted. The Fall prevents the individual from serving God through one's own ability. It does not mean that man is without free will. Individuals have freedom to choose between right and wrong. God can fittingly hold them morally responsible for their actions. What people cannot do, apart from divine grace, is to obey and please God so that they accomplish their own eternal salvation (Luke 18:9-14, 25-27).

Yet another biblical emphasis regarding sin, as seen in Psalm14 is that sin is universal. This concept is a matter of observation. Have you ever met anyone who professed to be morally perfect? Furthermore, the people we consider "good" are usually the first to confess their own sinfulness. All men and women, without exception, require salvation.

Every child born into this world falls into sin. Our sinful nature is found in everyone regardless of one's upbringing. Theologians call this concept *original sin*. Original sin is not a "thing" that is attached to a person. Rather it is an inherent condition of human nature. It is the result of the fact that we are a part of a race that is fallen. The notion of original sin has led many to ask, "Why should we be held accountable for something that is inborn?" The point here, which is made clear in Romans 3:23, is that "All have sinned and fallen short of the glory of God." Therefore we are in need of salvation, not only because Adam and Eve sinned, but because we also have sinned by our own will and through our own actions.

The inquiring mind may then ask, "Where did sin come from in the first place?" The Bible does not specifically explain the ultimate reason why moral evil should have its place in a world created and ruled by a loving God. It is reasonable to assume, however, that if God intended to create man with free will that He would also need to allow for good and evil to exist. If there is not a choice between good and evil, is there really a choice? The fact remains that our first parents chose to sin, and we also choose to commit sin.

III. Suffered under Pontius Pilate

"Greater love has no man than this, that a man lay down his life for his friends" (John 15:13). It seems clear that the real reason for Christ's death was that He pointedly challenged the pride, position, and interests of the religious authorities of His day. However, the legal responsibility for His execution rests upon the Roman administration of the Province of Judea (Luke 23:13-25). Thus He "suffered under Pontius Pilate." Regardless of the historical role of the Jews and of the Roman government, the spiritual guilt that crucified Christ is an aspect of universal guilt.

Let us examine the results and the meaning of Christ's suffering. As mentioned previously, the consequences of sin are twofold. It separates us from God, and it so overrules our nature that we are in moral bondage, a tragic situation! Herein lies the beauty of what is often looked upon as a shameful cross. Through the suffering Christ we can be reconciled to God, born again and receive a new nature. Perhaps this is why Paul described the work of Christ upon the cross as a ministry of reconciliation, "And you, who once were estranged and hostile in mind, doing evil deeds, he has now reconciled." (Col. 1:21-22a)

In order better to understand Jesus' marvelous work at Calvary, we look to the Old Testament. The concept of a divine sacrifice for sins may seem outdated in our day, but early Christians (primarily Jews who accepted Christ as Messiah) knew, as Paul wrote in Hebrews 9:22, that "without the shedding of blood there is no forgiveness of sins."

Sacrifices were a way of life for the ancient Jews. Ever since the Lord approved of Abel's offering of lambs from his flock, followers of God brought sacrifices to Him. Some possible ideas to help us understand the concept of sacrifice are these:

1. A man wishes to dedicate one of his possessions to God. He therefore offers some part of it to God, thus symbolically dedicating the whole.
2. A man realizes that all he has and is belongs to God and should be offered to Him. He therefore takes a highly significant object and sacrifices it as a sign of his self-offering to God.
3. To share a meal together unites us in the sacred bond of host and guest, and is the means of fellowship. One therefore provides a sacrifice, part of which is offered to God, and part of it is eaten by the worshippers, as a sacred meal of fellowship.

A sacrifice, then, is the God-appointed means whereby we may offer ourselves to God in dedication and obedience and hold fellowship with Him. All of the ceremonial laws and sacrifices we discover in the Old Testament are means to meet this end. Micah 6:6-8 is a prime example.

The one thing, however, that man cannot do is to obey God as He ought to be obeyed. Man alone cannot fulfill his part of the covenant (the binding agreement), therefore he is alienated from God (Jer. 31:32). God's Son came, as perfect man, to do what sinful man must, but cannot do by for himself. As one of us, Jesus offered His life of holy obedience to God as the supreme sacrifice (Mark. 8:31; 14:36; I Pet. 2:21-24). The truth about Jesus is a clear example of why the cross is the symbol of our faith. Christians view the cross as the turning point in history. Although we are unable to understand much of the majesty and mystery of Christ's death, Scripture makes several facets of His work clear. The New Testament emphasizes that the suffering and death of Christ was the victory of the power of God. It manifested the power of moral obedience and long-suffering love against all the evil forces that weigh upon mankind. Although the nature of our "enemies" varies from age to age, this belief is still relevant and gives power to the gospel message.

The Apostle Paul teaches that sinful man is in bondage to satanic intelligences, great and small (2 Cor. 4:4; Gal. 4:3). Christ, as man, put Himself into the sphere of influence of these forces that ultimately crucified Him (I Cor. 2:6-8). His resurrection was the mark of victory over them.

Mankind was also in bondage to the curse of the Law of Moses that had been placed upon everyone who was disobedient (Gal.3:10). The numerous rules 613 of the Pharisees attest to the Jews' fearful desire to obey God. Christ, however, made the burden of the law ineffective (Rom. 7:4; 10:4). He suffered the punishment marked out by the Mosaic Law through His submission to an accursed death (Gal. 3:13).

Two other enemies of mankind are sin and death. Christ in His crucifixion identified Himself with man in these experiences. As Peter explains, "He himself bore our sins in his body on the tree" (I Pet. 2:24). It has sometimes been said that the

Word was not only made flesh in the womb of Mary, He was made sin on the cross of Calvary." Surely this is why from that cross that our Lord cried, "My God, my God, why hast thou forsaken me?" (Mark 15:34). He accepted the load of our sins, and God, who is holy and cannot look on sin, turned away His face.

Now we can enjoy fellowship with God because the story did not end there. Christ emerged from this temporary separation with the words, "Father, into thy hands I commit my spirit" (Luke 23:46). The reconciliation He had come to win was completed. Christ had paved a path to God for all who would trust this Savior for themselves.

The Incarnation and the earthly life that followed it was an act of God making Himself one with the human race. Identification is the essential spiritual principle by which one man can hope to bear the moral burden and fight the moral battle of another. The following analogy helps to show this truth. A citizen realizes that his native land is about to be occupied by an invading army. Because of his position, he has a chance to escape, take his professional skill with him, and earn a comfortable living in another land. Or he may voluntarily choose to remain with his fellow citizens who are less fortunate than himself so that he may use his talents to organize their defense. By identifying himself with them, he is able to take upon himself a major share of their common struggle. That God in Christ chose to conquer the power of evil with this method of identification is a supreme pledge of His goodwill toward man, of His grace, His willingness to forgive, and His love.

It is sometimes asked: "What difference can a divine act performed in Jerusalem two thousand years ago make in the life of a person today?" Failure to answer this question satisfactorily is one reason why genuine Christianity does not make a deeper and wider impact. A connection between then and now depends upon the principle of the solidarity of the race.

The concept of "identification with Christ" may be expressed by considering I Corinthians 15:22, "For as in Adam all die, so also in Christ shall all be made alive." Genesis 2:7 and 19-33, describe Adam, which means *the man*, as the ancestor of the human race. In other words, Adam is the *type* of the race. He is the figure whose action represents what every human being has done. When Paul states that Adam disobeyed and brought upon himself death and alienation from God he is implying that mankind and every member of the race, has disobeyed and dies. In like manner, every one who by repentance, obedience, and faith, truly accepts oneness with Christ is "in Christ." Our Lord's action then represents man's action. And each shares in the blessings of Christ's action. Sharing in the blessings of Christ helps us to identify with Christ and makes Christianity genuine.

Chapter Seven

The Power and
The Wisdom

[I believe that] "the third day He rose again from the dead;
He ascended into heaven, and sitteth at the right hand
of God the Father Almighty"
(The Creed)

I. He Rose Again

Christ rose from the dead on the third day following His crucifixion. This is the central fact of our Christian faith. Christ Himself foretold His death and resurrection at least three times (Matt. 12:40; 16:21; 20:19). The message of the risen Christ was the theme preached by Peter, John, and Paul as well as other first-century Christians (Acts 4:10, 23:6). In the resurrection, we who believe are offered the hope of salvation. The effect of an unrisen Christ would be a dead faith (I Cor. 15:17).

It is interesting that the cross, which represents the horrible experience of crucifixion, should become the central symbol of the Christian message. In the first century this gruesome form of death was vivid to the citizens of the Roman world. A religion that worshiped a man who died on a cross was foolishness for many. It seemed safer and easier for them to worship the Roman emperor, as they were officially encouraged to do. Paul recognized the apparent foolishness of preaching the message of the crucified Christ (I Cor. 1:21-24). The main point of Paul's message is that Christ's resurrection brings freedom from sin and fullness of life (I Cor. 15:17-19). Thus, the cross has become the symbol of new life found through the Savior (John 3:14-16).

The victory that began on the cross is to be accepted by faith. Neither the ancient nor the modern mind can understand all of the aspects surrounding the resurrection of our Lord. Perhaps this is the reason why some Athenians "mocked" Paul "when they heard of the resurrection of the dead" (Acts 17:32). Likewise, modern people have sometimes chosen only to revere Jesus as a martyr for a good cause. In so doing, they must offer some other explanation for the miraculous resurrection of the physical body of Jesus.

Despite the apparent foolishness of believing in the efficacy of the Cross and the benefits of the Resurrection, this is the very core of our Christian faith. First-century Christians believed and taught this message. What follows is a summary of the biblical teaching concerning Christ's resurrection.

II. The Easter Event

Resurrection followed crucifixion as Christ had predicted. Jesus' crucifixion was recorded as an actual event, including His death and burial. In the same straightforward manner in which the death and burial is recorded, the resurrection is presented as a real event. Christ predicted that He would be handed over to the Gentiles to be crucified. Further, He predicted His victory over death on the third day (Matt. 20:19). Tradition maintains that Jesus died before sunset on Friday of Passover week. The Gospel narratives record that He then rose early on Sunday, the first day of the week. The Jews counted this period of time as three days (Acts 10:39-40).

Mary Magdalene, Mary the mother of James, and Salome first discovered the evidence of Jesus' resurrection. These close friends of Jesus intended to anoint His body with spices as preparation for proper burial (Mark 16:1; Luke 24:1).

How they were to roll away the large stone covering the tomb they did not know. These women arrived at the burial place, where they expected to find the body of Jesus. The angel who met them at the tomb told them to go and tell the disciples "that he has risen" (Matt. 28:7). Mary Magdalene, once possessed by demons, was the first person to see and talk with the risen Lord (John 20:11-18).

All the disciples later saw Him. He also appeared to Cleopas and his companion on the road to Emmaus. After they recognized Him, He vanished from their sight (Luke 24:13; 26-31). At another time while all the disciples except Thomas were in a room with the doors shut, Jesus appeared to them (John 20:19-25). Later Jesus stood among them when Thomas was present. Even this disciple, a noted doubter, believed that this was the same Jesus he had followed for three years (John 20:26-31). When Jesus appeared for the third time to His disciples, He ate with them (John 21:4-14).

The accumulated evidence from these accounts supports the belief that the resurrected body was also a "glorified" body in that He could appear in ways and places that He could not do before. Yet He could eat fish with them and be touched. The resurrection body was indeed the body that had died. Christ was not a disembodied spirit. Yet in His resurrected state He is now glorified.

The resurrection of Christ from the grave cannot be fully explained or understood by the inquiring mind of either skeptic or believer. Scriptural accounts are not written in such a way as to provide full scientific documentation for a supernatural event. Yet He was seen by His close disciples and later by a crowd of five hundred (I Cor. 15:6). These eyewitnesses who had lived and walked with Jesus before the crucifixion were convinced that Jesus had risen from the dead.

The resurrection of our Lord provides a confident hope for eternal life. As mortals, in ourselves we cannot reasonably believe we can become immortal or obtain eternal life. However, eternal life is possible because God raised Jesus from the dead. Eternal life is lifted from the level of an impossible hope to a promise from a God capable of delivering on that hope.

III. Evidence for the Resurrection

Belief in the resurrection of Jesus holds a central place in the Christian faith. What one believes about the Resurrection influences what one believes about the whole of Christianity. Critics of the miraculous resurrection commonly suggest that to accept this belief runs counter to the natural way of perceiving reality. To individuals already believing in the Resurrection, emotions are involved because they know the importance of this event in their faith. However, we must attempt to examine the historical evidence without allowing presuppositions to color the outcome of the investigations.

Historical accounts indicate that the Resurrection was preached from the beginning of Christianity. In the first sermon recorded in Acts, Peter proclaims that Jesus was raised from the dead (Acts 2:32). The crowd that heard this message could have proved this statement false by coming up with the dead body of Jesus. This was never done. The resurrection was preached in the same city shortly after it happened, not merely at some distant place centuries later when it would have been hard to verify the facts. Eleven out of the twelve apostles so firmly believed in the Resurrection that they were put to death for their belief. It is hard to understand how so many would die for a statement they knew was a lie. Furthermore, Jewish leaders not so much disputed the Resurrection as that they tried to invalidate and squelch the rise of Christianity. To argue that the account of the Resurrection was a story fabricated by the disciples, one would need to ignore the facts.

Changed lives are the most compelling evidence for a risen Savior. These changed lives are not isolated cases limited to first-century believers. Throughout history changed lives have represented an ongoing process that has made Christianity adaptable to all cultures. Because of the many witnesses to the Resurrection, an individual believer who experiences the power of the Resurrection can be assured that one is not the victim of a beautiful but unsubstantial illusion.

IV. He Ascended into Heaven

For forty days following the Resurrection, Christ remained on earth appearing to the disciples at different times. Christ was then seen ascending into heaven to be seated at the right hand of the Father (Acts 1:1-11; Rom. 8:34). This ascension completed Christ's earthly mission. Now He reigns in glory distributing the fruits of His victorious resurrection to His believers (Eph. 1:20-23).

It is important to remember that when God took on an earthly body, He was able to identify in all points with humanity (Heb. 4:14-5:3). Since Christ left the disciples after victoriously conquering death, it seemed as if He had deserted them. However, Christ's departure did not make God inaccessible to people. Rather it made Him more accessible to us because

Christ became our advocate. As the Gospel writer states, "we have an advocate with the Father" (I John 2:1). The hope of eternal life is all the more believable because Christ conquered death through the Resurrection.

Chapter Eight

The Spirit of the Lord

"I believe in the Holy Ghost"
(The Creed)

I. The Holy Ghost

The traditional creedal term, Holy Ghost, misleads some people into believing that the Christian faith includes belief in ghosts and goblins. Of course this is a misconception. Fortunately, it is mainly confined to young children and to those who are relatively unfamiliar with the Christian faith. When the still widely used King James Version was translated, the word ghost meant spirit. Accordingly, the term Holy Ghost is interchangeable with the term Holy Spirit.

The Holy Spirit is the third Person of the Godhead, or Trinity. The Holy Spirit is not an impersonal force; He is the working agent of the Father and the Son in the world. To put it in other words, the Holy Spirit is the One who carries out the work of God when He acts within space and time.

II. The Holy Spirit in the Old Testament

References to the Holy Spirit in the Old Testament are not so explicit or so numerous as they are in the New Testament. Nonetheless, the Old Testament contains a significant number of allusions to the work of the Holy Spirit. These gave the early Church Fathers a foundation for understanding the third Person of the Trinity. Several passages alluding to the Holy Spirit convey the idea that God is acting directly in the world through His Spirit. The Holy Spirit was God's creative hand in the origination of the universe (Gen. 1:2; Psa.33:6; Isa. 40:13). When the Spirit rested upon the prophets and heroes of Israel, these chosen ones were equipped and inspired so that they could achieve the specific goal God had set for them (Judg. 6:34; Ezek.11:5).

By directing the prophets, the Holy Spirit inspired them so that they stimulated the people of Israel to look forward to the messianic kingdom. This would be the day when God would grant a great outpouring of His Spirit on the Messiah and on all His people (Joel 2:28-29). The beginning of the fulfillment of these expectations was at the opening of Christ's ministry, when the Holy Spirit came upon Him (Mark 1:9-12).

III. The Pentecost Experience

The day of Pentecost, the Church's birthday, saw the outpouring of the Holy Spirit upon all those gathered in the Upper Room (Acts 1:14). When this timid group received the Holy Spirit's outpouring, they burst forth to proclaim boldly and with confidence that Jesus Christ is the Savior (Acts 2:17-38). These were mostly uneducated people, but under the direction of the Holy Spirit they could refute with courage the most educated men of their day. It was as if Jesus was with them again (Acts 4:13).

The Holy Spirit was not just resting upon only a few of the early Christians but upon every member of the Church. This general outpouring of God's Spirit fulfilled the prophecy found in Joel 2:28-29. The early members of the Church started referring to the Holy Spirit as being the Spirit of Jesus (Phil. 1:19; Gal. 4:6). They found that having the Holy Spirit with them was like having Jesus with them. They were experiencing anew the strength that they found in Jesus when He walked among them.

IV. The Church's Understanding of the Holy Spirit

The early Church wrestled with their understanding of the identity and ministry of the Holy Spirit. They were commonly experiencing the Holy Spirit in ways that did not occur in the Old Testament. Early Christians discovered with new certainty that the Holy Spirit is a divine Person in the same sense as God the Father and God the Son.

The Holy Spirit, like the Father, is not an impersonal force but is a part of the three-person God. The Holy Spirit is often called the Comforter or Advocate. When the King James Version was translated, the term *comforter* carried the idea of "to strengthen." He furnishes the Christian with spiritual and moral strength. As Jesus promised each of us, the Spirit provides the same power and guidance His disciples had when they walked with Him (John 14:15-17; 16:7; Acts 1:5, 8). The Spirit of Christ will continue to work in the hearts and minds of each believer until the end of time.

The Holy Spirit, the Spirit of God the Father and God the Son, represents the saving presence of God in the world. The saving work of Jesus Christ in the hearts of mankind and the Church is the work of the Holy Spirit. The Cross and the Resurrection are the bases for His action and evidences of His power. He is confronting mankind with the results of the Crucifixion and the Resurrection.

V. The Work of the Holy Spirit

The Holy Spirit works in many ways in the world and in the lives of God's people. Whenever and wherever the Father is working, the Son and the Holy Spirit are also working. The Holy Spirit equipped the early leaders of the Church for their tasks. He also developed the gifts of each believer so that each member would fit harmoniously into the body of Christ. The same task of equipping each member of the church, clergy and laypersons, is carried on today by the Holy Spirit so that the Church can confront the world.

The writers of the Bible were inspired and guided by the Holy Spirit in their writings. This is an example of God using a wide variety of people with differing skills for His purpose and glory. The Holy Spirit guides the Church today so that we can come to a fuller understanding of God's revelation. Especially does He help us apply the Word to the issues of the day.

The guidance of the Holy Spirit acts within the Church and within the life of each believer. He convinces us of our need before the experience of salvation to open ourselves to God and to accept Jesus as our Savior. For some this aspect of the Holy Spirit's work is dramatic; for others it is quite gentle.

When we accept Jesus Christ as our Savior, the Holy Spirit dwells within our personalities to give shape and direction to our lives. The Spirit helps us to grow spiritually by providing the power we need to do God's will. He enlightens our minds and guides our feet. Although the Spirit lives in us, He does not overrule our freedom of choice. We are able, if we choose, to ignore the Holy Spirit. He does not violate or restrict our free will.

The Spirit stirs and guides our prayer life (Rom. 8:26). He directs us in how and for what we should pray. He also works in us to confirm our adoption into God's family, thereby giving us assurance of our salvation (Rom. 8:14-17). God's Spirit bears witness to us that all is well with us spiritually.

The Holy Spirit leads men and women into the pastoral ministry and other branches of full-time Christian service. He also guides men and women into certain positions and professions that are not always directly related to the institutional church. And He guides laypeople to their work. Thus the Holy Spirit prepares and enables each of us to do the job to which God has called us. In these and many other ways the Holy Spirit is involved in every moment of the believer's life. The Spirit of God guides the Church in recognizing and deciding whom He is calling to the ministry. The Holy Spirit also operates through the ministering of the sacraments. In these events He can confront the participant and make these outward symbols of an inward condition into spiritual encounters with God for the believing Church.

VI. The Trinity

It is a mistake to believe that the concept of God and the Trinity can be simple and completely understood. God is so great that we cannot fully grasp and understand Him with our limited human minds. From the early days of the Church to the present, some people have been misled by oversimplified concepts in the attempt to understand God. This is an area in where cults commonly stray into error.

The early members of the Church did not begin with intellectual speculation to formulate the concept of the Trinity. Instead, they worked from their experience of having Jesus Christ with them and observing Him do only that which God can do. From their interactions with Jesus Christ and the Holy Spirit, as well as from Old Testament teachings, the early Church set down their understanding of God. In turn, this led to our present understanding of the Trinity.

The Trinity is comprised of three Persons, the Father, the Son, and the Holy Spirit. Underlying this teaching is the idea that God has made Himself known to us in a threefold way. God the Father is the creative and judging Person. Jesus Christ, God the Son, is the Word of God become man in order to bring salvation to us. The Holy Spirit is the Spirit and personal agent of the Father and the Son. Through the Spirit the Father and the Son work in the lives of men and women. These are the three "dimensions" by which God has chosen to reveal Himself to us, but it does not mean that God has fully revealed Himself in these three ways. God is still a great mystery to His creation.

The Church's long-held creedal teaching on the Holy Trinity reads, "one divine substance, three divine persons." This formula can be misleading if it is not properly understood because it can sound as if the Church worships three gods. "Substance" does not contain the common idea of a solid body having weight and size. Instead, substance has to do with the essential nature of the object without any material connotations.

The doctrine of the Trinity seems impossible for the human mind to fully comprehend. John Wesley addressed this matter in a letter written in 1760 to "a Member of the Society," one of Wesley's established groups of believers. Here he writes of his understanding of the Trinity. The mystery, he says, does not lie in the fact of three Persons. The mystery lies in "how they are one." He brushes aside any effort to understand a divine Mystery. "I believe the fact. As to the manner, [sic] (wherein the whole mystery lies,) I believe nothing about it." It remains for believers to be careful not to confuse the Three Persons with each other. :It [sic] is a mysterious providence," Wesley concludes.

The Trinity
An excursus by Dr. Dennis Kinlaw, general editor of the Assurance Series.

The doctrine of the trinity is the most basic doctrine of the Christian faith. It is in it that we come to understand the nature of Christ and the nature of the God of whom he is the Son and where our salvation lies. The Old Testament makes it clear that God is one (Deut. 6:4). Yet, Jesus says that he and the Father are one, that to see him is to see the Father, that to receive him is to receive the Father, and that to reject him is to reject the Father. Then Jesus does things that only God can do, like raise the dead and forgive sins. He permits Thomas to call him God and accepts worship from him. The big question for the early church then was, 'Who is Jesus?" He was obviously a human person because he was the child of Mary and had flesh and blood just like other humans. And, then, he died on the cross just as the two thieves who were with him died.

A strong case can be made that the most significant intellectual advance in human history came as the church wrestled with this question. They believed that in Christ the world had received a genuine revelation of the nature of God. It was not a discovery of human thought. Jesus was seen as the gift of the Father to reveal himself so that we can really know who God is and what he is like. They believed also that Jesus was the Savior, and they knew that only God could save. So the New Testament writers present Jesus as both human and divine, the God-Man. But what did this do to the unity of God?

They came to feel that in the oneness of God there was differentiation, differentiation that did not disturb the unity in the divine being. The key to this lies in the development of the concept of personhood. A person as the Church came to speak of the person of Christ did not mean an individual in separated identity. The term in the Christian creeds means 'one whose completeness is in another'. The term as used in the classical creeds of the Church for the Father, the Son, and the Spirit means one who finds his source and identity in another.

One cannot be a Father without a child, so in a sense God's Son is the one who makes the Father the Father. One cannot be a child without having a Father, so the Father is the one who gives the Son his sonship. The same can be said of the Spirit, who is the Spirit of the Father and the Spirit of the Son. So the early church concluded that the Son is not all there is of God, but that all there is of God is in the Son. The same can be said of the Father and the Spirit.

The importance of this for our understanding of God and salvation cannot be overestimated. This means that God is not a single solitary will whose defining characteristic is omnipotence, Rather,

God is a being whose inner essence is interpersonal love. Love is an interpersonal relationship. This means then that love is not just something God does. It is what he is! (I John 4:8,16). This is expressed in the fact that the life of the Son is a gift of the Father's life to the Son. He is the only 'begotten' Son. His life comes from the Father. And the life of the Spirit is the same. His life is drawn from the Father and the Son.

The doctrine of the trinity is the basis also of the doctrine of salvation as well. We know that there is no salvation in us nor is there anything saving in anything that we do. We are where the problem is. In fact, we are the problem. Only God can save. But we also know that the salvation must take place where it is, that is in us. The problem is not in God. So how do we get the answer to where the problem is? Without the doctrine of the trinity there would be no answer. God could not leave his throne to come die on the cross if there were no 'differentiation' in the Godhead. Because of the trinity the Father can send the Son to become one of us, take the human problem into himself, and solve it in an eternal redemption. Because of the fact that God in his oneness is triune the human problem and the divine answer could meet in the God-Man, in Jesus Christ, son of Mary and Son of God.

Can we understand all of this? No! It is not surprising that to those who know him, God is beyond our comprehension: perhaps this why Paul insists on calling it all a great mystery Rom. 16:25-26). But it is not a mystery that repels us. It is a mystery that allures us because it is the mystery of ultimate love, God's love. So, we prostrate ourselves and worship. As the seraphim in Isaiah's vision (6:3) found God trice holy, we can join with them in their song. Little wonder that the natural expression of benediction in the New Testament is in the name of the triune God: "May the grace of the Lord Jesus Christ, and the love of God, and the fellowship of the Holy Spirit be with you all" (II Cor. 13:14).

Chapter Nine

The People of God

[I believe in] "the Holy Catholic Church"
(The Creed)

I. The Church: A Divine Plan

One foundation principle is that the Church draws its existence from the eternal will of God (Eph. 3:1-12). Established by God, the Church is His living body expressing both unity and diversity. The Christian community is necessary to the Christian faith. An essential part of being a Christian is to be incorporated as a baptized believer into the Church. For those who are in the church as members, the unity of our faith opens our eyes to our need for one another while the bond of love, which enables us to transcend the obvious diversities, nourishes our faith. The Christian faith, then, has both personal and corporate dimensions. God works in our lives, sometimes as individuals, and sometimes as members of His Church.

The relationship between individual and corporate worship is illustrated by the use of the means of grace. The means of grace are understood as specific acts of worship to receive God's grace. These acts include personal devotion, morality, public worship, fellowship with believers, study of the Bible, preaching of the gospel, and partaking of the sacraments. These prepare us for and lead us into fellowship with God. Some of us think of the means of grace as a kind of inward and personal soul walk with God. Yet, grace cannot be separated from the Church because there are appointed means of grace that are found only within the Church.

The Church is truly made up of "one body and one Spirit, . . . one Lord, one faith, one baptism" (Eph. 4:4, 5). Therefore, all Churches are one because of our belief in the Trinity, the Creation, the Incarnation, the person of Christ, the Atonement and Resurrection, and the Holy Spirit. The reason for differences today lies in the diversity of human temperament and differing human experiences, whereas God is always the same.

The people of God make up the visible as well as the invisible Church. The visible Church is the organized body of believers by profession of faith and by holy baptism. The invisible Church is the whole company of those, known only to God, who are united to Christ by faith. Ideally the two, (the visible Church and the invisible Church) are the same. This was the thought of the first-century Church (Acts 2:38; 10:47; 22:16). The possibility of there being Christian believers outside the body of the Church is not considered in the New Testament. Unworthy and disorderly members of a local church are not considered as outsiders, but are left to God's judgment (Heb. 6:4-6; 10:29-30).

The "communion of saints" refers to the belief that all who are united with Christ are a part of His body in love and faith. The Church is not to be divided because of race, culture or language differences. The Church is one in Christ (Acts 10:34-35; Gal. 3:27-29; Col. 3:10-11). The deeper sense of the phrase "the communion of saints" affirms that the one Church is not divided even by death because the universal Church is made up of both living and non-living Christians. The recognition of the wider communion of saints is vital to the spiritual dignity of the Church.

II. The Church of the Old Covenant

From the beginning, God has declared Himself through a distinct community. The strong convictions of the early Church affirmed the continuity of the Christian Church with the faithful of Israel. The Jewish holy books were read in early Christian worship and quoted as authoritative. *Church* in the New Testament is the same as "the congregation of Israel" used in the Old Testament, which is the story of God's revelation in history (Acts 7:37-38).

III. The Church of the New Israel

The Christian Church in the New Testament can be seen as the new Israel (Gal. 6:16). Those who were true and faithful to Christ became the new Church. Because they followed God's leading, the divine destiny of Israel was fulfilled. To this small group of believers was added all who confessed Jesus Christ as Lord (Acts 2:47b). Therefore, the new Church is the continuation of the Old Covenant.

Certain outward signs of faith in Christ identify Christian believers. These include church membership and the moral discipline of the Christian life. Christ's atonement freed the believer from the Jewish law and provided a new covenant of obedience through inner spiritual power. God promised through Jeremiah that when He visited His people, there would be a new covenant of inward spirituality. This event brought us victorious power to obey the law of God from the heart (Jer. 31:33-34; Heb. 10:1-25).

The rise of the Church corresponds to its heritage. John the Baptist (Jewish prophet and Christian saint) was the connecting link between Judaism proper and the distinctive Christian Church. The Gospels show that his preaching ministry marks the beginning of the Christian movement (Mark 1:1-8). John's followers formed the nucleus from which the Church was drawn (John 1:34-42). The early Christians connected Christian baptism with John's baptism. Therefore, in one sense, the Church grew out of a small, awakened group of Israelites.

We believe that our Lord Jesus Christ founded the Church. His actions and words clearly point to the idea of His disciples being the new Israel. As such they were a disciplined community characterized by Christlikeness. The early church corresponding to the old Israelite congregation, continues the Passover feast in the form of the communal meal (Luke 22:14-20).

The Church is "the bride of Christ." The Lord as husband to His people is a frequent Old Testament figure (Isa. 62:4-5). Therefore, idolatry is referred to as adultery (Jer. 3:6-10; Eze. 23:36-49; Hos. 2:2-5). This parallel is applied to the new Israel. The Church is the bride of Christ. The intimate union in spirit that exists between the Lord and His Church is compared to marriage (Eph. 5:23-32; Rev. 21:2-3, 9).

The body of Christ is also a term applied to the Church. This term is chiefly associated with the writings of Paul (I Cor. 12:4-31a). In his appeal for love and unity in the church, Paul points out that Christians have a variety of spiritual gifts. Though some gifts are more prominent than others, all are necessary for the fulfilling of God's plan. The different members are comparable to various limbs and organs of the human body with some members being more important or "honored" than others. Yet each is necessary to the total health of the group as are the organs of the body. In this way, the entire church may be the healthy body of Christ (Eph. 4:1-16).

IV. The Marks of the Church

The marks of the Church are fourfold. The first is oneness. *1*
There is but one God who has shown His saving grace in Christ.
This grace is mediated by one Spirit. Therefore, there is only
one Church. Oneness is disguised by many competing denominations, yet the unity exists in the mind of God and in the
prayers and hopes of faithful Christians. Believers are not baptized into separate denominations of which they are members
but into the one Church (Eph. 4:4-6).

The second mark of the Church is the fact that it is holy. *2*
This biblical term means "separate to God, for His own use."
This does not mean that all its members lead pure lives. The
Church is different because it is founded by God and not by
man. The purpose of the Church is to fulfill God's plan of sal-
vation for all people (Eph. 3:3-6, 9-11; I Pet. 2:9).

The third mark of the Church is that it is "catholic," which *3*
means universal. The use of the term *catholic* indicates the
Church is worldwide and not isolated into one section or region
of the earth. The gospel is the universal message of the Church.
It can be trusted in all human experiences.

The fourth mark of the Church is that it is "apostolic." The *4*
Church now existing is the same Church as the apostolic
Church originally founded by Christ. The same faith has been
maintained from that day to this. This continuity of the Church
denies the idea that one can form a "new" Church founded by
another leader who claims to replace Christ.

V. The Ministry of the Church

An important aspect of the ministry of the Church is the
priesthood of all believers. The priest of the Old Testament represented the people to God. He directed their worship and
enabled them to approach God. It is the New Testament belief

that all believers can approach God. Therefore, the whole Church is a "royal priesthood" (I Pet. 2:9).

The minister is the representative priest in the Church. The ministry is a special limb of the priestly body. Christ uses the Church as His instrument to administer the gospel and the sacraments. A Christian minister, accordingly, acts under the authority of Christ.

As we are all sinners saved by grace, no one is worthy to administer the sacraments. One's authority lies in the fact that Christ has called the person to ministry. Therefore, the first stage for becoming a minister of the Gospel is the calling of the Holy Spirit (Acts 13:2). The Church does not call the minister but affirms the call, which the minister has received from God.

Today, the church has become institutionalized with several forms of authority and governing agencies. In the first century, this institutionalization did not exist. The church consisted of groups of believers, commonly meeting in houses. The church was one in spirit rather than in organization. As Christians were permitted more freedom to worship, the church became more formally structured. However, a believer's first love should always be for the spiritual dimension of the Church as the Body of Christ and not the church government.

It is important that the ordained minister and the layperson remember that they are coworkers in the eyes of God. All Christians are called into the ministry of the Church in order to supply each other's needs. Through the act of servanthood, every believer is to glorify God, the supplier of all needs. Therefore, the clergy should not hold their ordination or diplomas of higher education over the heads of the laity as a sign of superiority, but of service. The ministry of the church is most effective when all believers are equally committed to the outreach of the gospel.

Chapter Ten

The Means of Grace

I. Grace and the Means of Grace

God's saving action toward His Church and toward individuals demonstrates His divine grace. In brief, divine grace is God's undeserved favor toward humanity. Although helpless to save ourselves, we are saved by God's grace. We do cooperate with God by trusting in His grace alone, and not in our actions to earn salvation. The experience of Christians demonstrates that the means of grace are certain stated, regular, and divinely promised channels through which God bestows His favor, e.g., worship, baptism, and Holy Communion. Although attending church, having devotions, being baptized, and partaking of Holy Communion are visible signs of our inward experience of God's grace, we do not earn God's grace through these actions. We can be confident of receiving God's grace because He has faithfully promised to give His grace to those seeking Him with all their hearts (Jer. 29:13).

II. Worship

Worship is the action of believers working together to express the faith and love that God has given to the Church. The purpose of worship is to give God the praise and reverence He deserves and to build up the Church in love and faith. Principal elements of worship include adoration, praise, confession of sin, profession of faith, and intercession. Worship through prayer, meditation and Bible reading should be carried out both as individuals and as a body of believers. Worship is an outward sign of our inward devotion. True worship in our hearts confirms and strengthens what we know in our head. Many forms of worship may be used to deepen our awareness of God, for example, hymns, songs, prayer, preaching, and Scripture reading. Corporate worship is not the assembling of people to influence one another; rather it is the gathering of believers in the presence of the Lord. When the people of God worship together, God is in their midst (Matt.18:20). The Holy Spirit works through our participation in worship to bring to us a power that is not our own.

Preaching informs and educates the worshiping Church by making clear the definite beliefs of personal faith. The purpose of preaching is to paint a vivid portrait of the living Lord. This is more than the sermon. The picture can also be painted by reading the Scripture, partaking of the sacraments, singing hymns, and reciting the creeds. Preaching as a means of grace uses Holy Scripture, the testimony of the Church's faith, and the preacher's own testimony to present Christ to the people. The Holy Spirit works through this testimony so that the listener hears not only the words of the preacher but also the words of Christ.

As an act of worship, intercessory prayer asks for God's blessing and assistance in daily affairs for others. Petition asks this for us. The purpose of prayer is not to remind God of human needs or to change God's mind. Its purpose is the enabling of the praying Church to become a more fully sensitive, obedient, and useful instrument of God for the accomplishment of His will. As Christians, we pray as a natural result of our confidence in God's goodness and wisdom. Through prayer we learn both dependence upon God and confidence in asking.

These expressions of worship are not magic. They are means of grace dependent upon divine promise and the worshiper's cooperation. Likewise the Christian sacraments of baptism and Holy Communion are God-centered and the foundation of the worshiper's confident hope of divine blessing.

III. The Sacramental Principle

Worship involves the use of symbolism. A symbol that is seen and handled has more power to move one's imagination than the spoken word alone. A sacrament is a symbol involving active participation and spoken words based on the principle that God can bring about the spiritual through the physical.

The use of symbolism does not indicate a lack of spirituality. Christianity teaches that God created the physical universe, filled it with spiritual meaning, has contact with it, uses it, and works through it to accomplish His purposes. The sacraments are a means of grace. When partaken in faith they convey to us a sense of security with God. This security is not dependent upon the automatic performance of an act, but upon the sincere and thoughtful intentions of following the Lord's example (I Cor. 11:25).

IV. Holy Baptism

Holy Baptism signifies one's initiation into the Christian life and community. This sacrament symbolizes self-identification with Christ, incorporation into the Church, and the gift of the

Holy Spirit (John 3:5). Baptism in the triune name signifies that the baptized person yields himself/herself to the possession and authority of God who made Himself known as Father, Son, and Holy Spirit. By tradition, the use of water and the triune name of God are essential to Holy Baptism. Water is used in baptism to symbolize the cleansing of sins and a new life. We identify with the dying Christ's act of suffering love and with the risen Christ's triumph (Rom. 6:3-6).

V. Holy Communion or Eucharist

As baptism is one's first symbolic identification with Christ, Holy Communion is the continuing and ever-renewed identification of the believer with the Lord. Among Christians this sacrament is commonly known as the Lord's Supper, Holy Communion, and the Mass. It is properly called *the Eucharist*. The word simply means "thanksgiving." In the New Testament, the Eucharist is clearly associated with the Passover. It proclaims that the Messiah has come, bringing the promised kingdom by His death and resurrection. The Eucharist celebrates our reception of the Divine life and our deliverance from the power of sin, just as the Passover celebrated the Israelites' deliverance from the power of Pharaoh (Ex. 12). Thus we share in Christ's death and resurrection. The Eucharist is not only the supreme means of communion between the faithful and their Lord; it is the means of the communion of all the faithful with one another. Christians joining together in the sacrament demonstrate the unity of the Church.

The doctrine of the Real Presence (held by some Christian communions) affirms the experience of the Church in perceiving the "presence" of Christ in worship. It means that at a specific time and place our Lord reveals Himself to certain persons.

Chapter Eleven

The Written Word

I. The Witness to the Christ-Centered Faith

Christian worship, as earlier observed, is centered upon Jesus Christ. Christ Jesus is both a historical person and a living presence. That is, He was born, lived, spoke, died and rose again, and yet continues to live in our lives today. His death and resurrection brought into the world a divine power that cannot be scientifically explained.

Believing in the facts about the historical Jesus does not automatically lead to salvation, but it is a foundation of faith. For example, even though many people experienced the actual events with Jesus, if they did not accept Him as the Messiah they were not saved. To become a Christian, one must be confronted by the living Christ in a personal experience that results in a faith that He is truly the Lord of all. While this experience is individual and personal, nevertheless, our faith has a firm foundation because it is grounded in the historical account of Jesus. The Bible records for us the Church's knowledge of the facts about Christ and portrays His personality.

II. The Inspiration of the Bible

Inspiration is the power of our mind and spirit coming alive by the indwelling of the Holy Spirit. This enables us more fully to understand and to declare the revelation, which God is making known. The writers of the Old and New Testaments were inspired by God when they recorded the events of the Bible. Therefore, the authority of the Bible is founded upon its content, not upon the author's style. The supremacy of the Bible lies in the fact that it is the primary and sufficient witness of Christ.

The Holy Scriptures contain all that is necessary for our knowledge of God's holy and sovereign will, Jesus Christ the only Redeemer, our salvation, and our growth in grace. The Scriptures are the guide and final authority for the faith and conduct of individuals and for the doctrines and life of the Church. Anything contrary to the teachings of the Scriptures opposes the purposes of God, and, therefore, should be carefully questioned, and rejected, by the body of Christ. The Holy Spirit inspired the authors and caused them to perceive Gods truth and record it with accuracy. He has preserved the Scriptures through the long process of hand copying and translating them. The Scriptures are the primary source for the Church's teaching, preaching, witnessing, identifying error, correcting faults, and training believers for the ministry (2 Tim. 3:14-17).

III. The Canon of Scriptures

The word *canon* means a standard, a rule of faith. The canon of Scripture is the list of books recognized by the Church as authoritative. Because the Bible is canonical, it is read in the Church as a part of Christian worship and used to establish basic Christian beliefs. The conviction that certain books are authoritative is grounded upon the principle of inspiration. That is, in addition to guiding the writers, the

Holy Spirit guided the Church in the selection of the canonical books.

The writers of Scripture wrote knowing that the Holy Spirit was moving them to record what was spiritually important. Individually, they did not regard their writings as being too different from other writers of their day. They were not writing with a goal of creating a canon. However, as time passed, these books found greater appeal among the people of God as expressing the essentials of the faith. Gradually, respect for them increased to the extent that the Church gave them their place of primary importance. The choosing of certain books as authoritative was not, and should not be, regarded as censorship for it was done under the guidance of the Holy Spirit.

The Old Testament was established when a group of rabbis agreed that certain group of writings were canonical. The Pentateuch (Genesis, Exodus, Leviticus, Numbers, and Deuteronomy) was accepted by 400 B. C. The historical and Prophetic books were accepted by 200 B. C. The "Sacred Writings" (Psalms, Proverbs, Song of Solomon, Lamentations, and Ecclesiastes) were accepted as canonical by about 100 B. C.

The Apocrypha, which means "hidden things," is a collection of books written during the time between the last writings of the Old Testament and the initial writings of the New Testament. These books are regarded by the Protestant church as noteworthy, but not canonical. They are significant because they record the history of the Jewish people during this intertestamental period.

A similar process of canonization took place with the New Testament. When the New Testament uses the term "the Scriptures" it refers to the Old Testament (2 Tim. 3:16). The early church viewed the Old Testament, the words of Jesus, and the writings of the apostles as having authority. During the first century, the New Testament writings were recognized as a substitute for the personal presence of an apostle. As time passed, certain writings gained a distinct place and were read with the Old Testament in Christian worship. By the fourth century, our present New Testament was firmly established.

IV. The Old Testament Scriptures

The importance of the Old Testament is that it is a history of the preparation of the chosen people of God for the coming of Christ. Christianity includes thoughts, ideals and morals, but it is basically a religion of redemption, founded on the way God has acted on our behalf through history. Thus, Christianity is rooted in history. Critics at times have asserted that the Bible is historically unreliable. But more recent historical and archaeological research continues to provide evidence that these claims are false.

Parts of the New Testament must be understood in terms of the Jewish tradition because the writers of the New Testament were from the Jewish culture. Thus, their writings were influenced by that heritage. For example, phrases such as "the righteousness of God" can be properly understood only when compared to their Old Testament usage.

God's chosen people were led out of Egypt as slaves, where they had lived in a religious culture that worshiped many gods. While wandering in the wilderness, they had a difficult time abandoning their habits of idol worship. Although they were instructed by Moses and Aaron, God's appointed prophets, they continually disobeyed God's commandments. However, God was patient and continued to reveal His character and will to His people through the voices of the prophets and through His mighty acts.

This can be compared to our development of a friendship. We do not learn everything about a person at the initial meeting. As we spend time with a person, we learn more about the individual's character and personality. In most friendships there are times when we do not understand the other person, but as we continue to seek to develop the relationship, the friendship continues to grow deeper. So it is with God and His people. Even as they continued to disobey, God persevered in making Himself known to them. The Old Testament is the record of this process.

The Jewish people had a vivid sense that God was real; hence religion was a matter of immense concern. God was sovereign, majestic, active, and near. Thus, when a Jew disobeyed God, he had an intense awareness that he was sinning, not merely against social custom, but against a mighty and holy God.

The entire Old Testament canon is properly used both as a personal and corporate worship source. To some, the history and law contained in the Old Testament may not seem devotionally stimulating, but they are beneficial as a measuring rod for comparing life's experiences to God's standards. The poetry and prophecy sections are more popular because they involve the emotions and deeper feelings of the writer and reader.

God's greatest revelation of Himself to His chosen people was through His incarnation in Jesus, the son of the Virgin Mary. This revelation fulfills much of the Old Testament prophecy. The Old and New Testaments are interrelated and are to be read and understood as reflecting on each other.

One of the first issues facing the early church was how it should preserve its link with its Jewish past. The center of this conflict was the role of the Old Testament for the Christian Church. It seems a fair judgment that a majority of leaders recognized the Old Testament as fully normative. Early Christians lived in near proximity to the culture and times of the Old Testament, thus they enjoyed a distinct advantage in understanding the import of its message. Today the Old Testament is properly seen as part of God's written revelation of Himself. This written revelation was completed in the New Testament.

V. New Testament Scripture

The most important emphasis of the Bible is the historic witness it gives to Jesus. One of the functions of an apostle was to testify of his personal firsthand experience with our Savior. As these personal friends of Jesus died, the unique office of apostleship came to an end. In due time, the Church recognized their apostolic writings, which now compose our New Testament, as inspired by the Holy Spirit and therefore authoritative for Christian faith and practice.

The purpose of these writings was evangelistic. The apostles chose various events from the life of Jesus with a clear purpose. Each story was specifically chosen with the related aims of winning people to Christ, of instructing them, of encouraging them, and of uplifting the body of believers in the faith.

There is no claim that the four Gospels compose a complete biography of the life of Jesus. The apostles, knowing that their historical roots were preserved in the Old Testament, sought to share Jesus' life and teaching by recording them for the people of God. Since no body of substantiated data has been found that discredits the events recorded, the Apostles' testimony stands. While the New Testament authors' purpose in writing was evangelical rather than biographical, the events of Jesus' life are in no way misrepresented.

The Christian faith is not centered in moral and spiritual practices but in the Person of Jesus Christ and the salvation He offers. His teachings emphasize love and forgiveness. As Christians, we regard His teachings as the cornerstone of our faith. He excels all other teachers. One of the main reasons certain sections were included in our Bible was that they provide "a word from the Lord" for guidance and discipline.

A key issue of modern New Testament scholarship is historical accuracy. The Christian religion depends upon these historical facts concerning Christ, although today some of these truths have been questioned. While some consider discussion concerning the Bible's reliability as unnecessary, such discussions can strengthen our faith. Some scholars ask such questions as, "Are the Gospels reliable history?" If there are interpretive touches, how many? Did the Bible come out of the believing mind and experience of the Church, or did it emerge from the imaginings of the early group in order to symbolize their faith? Three guides have been suggested for dealing with these questions: consistency, majesty, and continuity.

The Consistency of the Gospels: Although the Gospels come from different backgrounds, traditions and attitudes, there is always a unity in the portrayal of Christ. If the accounts of Christ's life were merely the imaginings of the Gospel writers, it is not likely that the content of the Gospels would be unified. But, such is not the case. The information that has come down through the centuries, despite many attempts to distort its message, has consistently retained a unified character.

The Majesty of the Gospels: Jesus Christ is a magnificent figure in history. He has won the admiration even of those who do not believe in Him. It is unlikely that the small group of ordinary people who wrote the Gospels could have done so without divine inspiration. The Gospel writers simply recorded some of the events of their lives with Jesus.

The Continuity of Christian Thought: The principle of continuity refers to the assumption that the confession of Christian thought, which has held firm through the centuries, also held during the period of time between the life of our Lord and the formation of the written Gospels. The strong suggestion of this principle is that New Testament Christians understood their Lord and were therefore reliable witnesses to His life and ministry.

Chapter Twelve

The Double Cure

[I believe in] "the forgiveness of sins"
(The Creed)

I. Personal Religion

The Apostles' Creed thus far has centered on the facts of the Christian faith: such as Jesus's birth, death, and resurrection. There is also a personal dimension to our faith that grows out of these facts. The message of God's revelation can make a real difference to human beings only if it appeals to both thoughts and feelings and results in positive response. The historical facts (head knowledge) and personal response (heart knowledge) must be kept in balance so that faith becomes neither an academic exercise nor a sentimental emotional high.

This balance is maintained as the grace of God is manifested through the Holy Spirit in the hearts of individual believers today. While the Holy Spirit works in individuals, it is important to remember that individuals are not isolated and that the Spirit works to keep both the individual and the body of Christ in harmony and balance.

Although God is consistent in character and will, human nature varies. Consequently, our loving God deals with us individually. It should not surprise us that while the Church is united in its beliefs about God and Christ, its members are not so united in their personal beliefs about religious experience. Therefore it is necessary not only to define the words that different Christian denominations use, but also to understand them. This understanding promotes peace and unity in the Church and leads to a better understanding of the gospel.

The study of personal religion has two parts, the doctrine of grace and the doctrine of the life of Christian grace. The doctrine of grace is concerned about how God seeks to know and bring about the salvation of humankind. The doctrine of the life of Christian grace focuses on how a person's heart responds to God's seeking.

II. Doctrine of Grace

The central idea of grace is that it is the undeserved favor of God. This means that God loves His people not because they earn or deserve His love but because He is love and desires to save them Deut. 7:7-8; Matt. 20:1-16). An accompanying aspect of this grace is that it is an action that God initiates to bring about His will. That is, God's grace enables persons to respond to His love. Anyone who truly believes in God is the recipient of grace.

We can choose to turn to God in response to His grace that demonstrated His desire to have a relationship with us, His Spirit enables us to respond. Thus, we are completely dependent upon God our Creator and Master for our salvation (John 15:16).

Roman Catholics believe that one is saved by grace in that God must make the first move. However, in response to every act of God, Catholics believe they must freely cooperate or they will miss their final salvation. This is often referred to as salvation by grace and works. Martin Luther and the Reformers reacted strongly against this belief and stated that salvation is "by grace alone." The reason for the Reformer's stand is that they wanted to uphold the position that there is nothing saving in human actions in and of themselves. Only God can save. But when we open to his knock and His life enters into us, His life within us manifests itself in works of love.

St. Augustine of Hippo (354-430) was a highly respected teacher in the Church. He systematized the Church's beliefs on such things as the Church, the ministry, and the sacraments within the Catholic tradition. The name given to his system is "Augustinianism." Augustine offered a highly organized system of beliefs about divine grace, conversion, the experience of personal religion, and the hope of salvation. His teaching emphasizes that God's grace alone is responsible for one's final salvation but that mankind is the instrument of God's action. John Calvin, one of the Protestant reformers, embraced Augustinianism as the basis for the system of beliefs we call Calvinism.

Both Augustinian and Calvinistic thought emphasize total depravity, the bondage of the will and the guilt of original sin. Taken together, these doctrines imply that mankind deserves to be eternally separated from God because of the Fall. Augustinian/Calvinistic thought embodies several teachings about grace: election, predestination, irresistible grace, final perseverance, and reprobation.

Election affirms that God knows the total human situation, and chooses some persons and nations to play a particular part in history. Particular election teaches that God chooses certain individuals to receive his grace. Predestination suggests that

God has known from the beginning of time those he was going to choose to be saved. God's grace to the elect is sovereign, implying that the elect will always come to know Him. Therefore, God's grace is described as irresistible. Final perseverance means that those who receive the gift of faith will continue in this state of grace throughout their physical lives and they will be given eternal life at death. Reprobation is the opposite of election. The reprobates are the ones God has chosen to be condemned.

Arminianism is a Protestant school of thought that followed a strong tradition rooted in the writings of the early Church fathers that rejected the concepts of particular election and reprobation and recognized an element of contingency. Arminianism emphasizes the view that salvation by grace is offered universally. The line from the well-known gospel song, "Whosoever will may come," clearly expresses this key Ariminian concept. Jacobus Arminius (1560-1609), a Dutch theologian, revived and organized this interpretation of the Scriptures. John Wesley (1703-1791) called himself an "Arminian." Wesley emphasized salvation by grace and justification by faith. However, he opposed the notions of particular election, predestination, and reprobation. These related distinctions constitute one of the more significant contributions of the Methodist movement to the Church's theology.

John Wesley enriched our understanding of this tradition with the concept of prevenient grace. The word prevenient is an old English word that means "coming before." The God of all grace is the God who searches for the sinner even before the sinner thinks of seeking God. When He finds the sinner, God through His Spirit offers grace to respond to God's offer of salvation.

Universal Grace is the belief that God's grace is available to all, suggesting that God seeks each person to respond to Him. The ultimate responsibility for whether a person responds favorably to God's offer of grace rests therefore upon the individual, not upon God's eternal decree. Thus it is said that everyone has free will.

III. Life of Grace

Christian nurture and conversion are two aspects of describing how one comes to respond to God's initiative and becomes a Christian. Christian nurture, as a pathway to faith, begins with infant dedication (or in some traditions, infant baptism), family prayers, Christian education, worship, and devotional discipline. Many believers have lived their Christian lives in this way. At some point in time, the individual accepts as fact that Christ died for "me" and responds to this manifestation of God's love. This response is called conversion. True conversion brings with it a conscious awareness that all things have become new. Sometimes this awareness may be a result of one's devotional discipline; it may also be a response to a direct evidence of God's grace. However it occurs, conversion results when head knowledge becomes heart knowledge. However it occurs, conversion results when head knowledge and heart knowledge meet in transforming power. Thus Christian nurture and conversion complement each other. From this perspective, then, a personal decision is necessary to experience saving grace. It logically follows that devotional disciplines maintain and enrich a Christian's personal relationship with Christ.

The "religion of law" is religion based on the recognition of man's duty to obey God's will and please Him. The law, then, was the relationship that the Israelites had with God as recorded in the Old Testament. Further, an awareness of the law is needed for understanding the ethical and holy character of God, the seriousness of sin in His sight, and the importance of obeying His commandments. Finally, the law is the foundation for understanding grace and the forgiveness of sins.

"Preaching the Law" is necessary so people can sense their need of grace and seek it. Through preaching, a person comes to see one's self clearly as a sinner and is prepared to accept from God that which one can never do for one's self or hope to repay. Persons see that they cannot meet God's standards in their own strength and that they will never deserve forgiveness. This realization is called "conviction of sin." It is the first step in one's Christian experience.

The second step in Christian experience occurs when a person, having been confronted with the moral and spiritual law of God, decides to accept God's invitation to belief. Such an individual desires to turn away from disobedience. This desire results in repentance, itself a gift from God (Acts 11:18; II Tim. 2:25).

Faith is the response to God's offer of forgiveness and a new life for the sinner who repents. It is union with God in loving personal trust. It is based on reasoned truth (Rom. 10:17) and personal experience. This kind of faith brings about a new relationship that involves all of one's life. The essential element of faith is trust in the love and power of God as made known to man in the death and resurrection of Jesus Christ. This means that Christ becomes the central Person in one's life (Col. 3:3-4, 11). This personal experience results from the work of the Holy Spirit in enabling a person to respond to God's grace with an open and willing heart (I Cor. 12:3).

Justification is God's response toward us when we unite ourselves with Him by faith in Christ. It results in the forgiveness of our sins and our acceptance with God. The person who is justified is welcomed into God's loving arms just as a new baby is welcomed into the arms of loving parents. For example, a child does not do anything special to earn its parents' acceptance. They simply give it. We do not earn God's acceptance; we only receive it by faith.

Justification, then, is a legal term expressing God's response to a person's faith and indicates the legal standing of the person before God. Regeneration, a related concept, is the beginning of a new pattern of a changed life within us. God in response to our faith creates in us a life pleasing to Himself by giving us the Holy Spirit. The Holy Spirit dwells in us and changes our hearts, minds, and wills so that we may please God. The term "born again" is used to describe this experience (John 3:5, 7).

Justification is what God does for us and regeneration is what God does in us. The apostle Paul describes this new life of the Christian as adoption (Rom. 8:15; Gal. 4:5-6). Through adoption, a Christian shares with Christ the privilege of going to the Father just as an adopted child has all the privileges of going to its new parents.

As an adopted child may wonder how one can be certain of one's family status, a Christian may wonder about the assurance of one's salvation. The various branches of the Church have given several answers.

The Roman Catholic Church teaches that a faithful Christian cannot be certain of salvation until arrival at a godly and believing death. One should not doubt God's promises, but neither should one assume that one will not fall from grace. The Calvinist or Reformed position relative to assurance is based upon the belief in election and perseverance. A person is a chosen object of God's irresistible grace and, by definition, cannot leave it. John Wesley taught that the saving relationship is a personal one and that it can never be frozen in this life, but that it is possible for the believer to have a full assurance or certainty of a personal relationship with God. He taught that it is impossible to doubt salvation if one personally experiences an inward change of will and an outward change of lifestyle (I John 2:3, 5, 29). The believer may also be certain of one's relationship because of the activity of the Holy Spirit in all areas of one's life. Wesley called this activity the "witness of the

Spirit." He taught that this assurance does not allow the believer to assume that one cannot fall from grace. Rather, Wesley taught that the believer has confidence as he or she maintains a life of faith in discipline and moral integrity in personal fellowship with God.

Sanctification begins with regeneration and leads to a state of completeness in Christ. Sanctification cannot be accomplished by the efforts of the believer but is the fruit of the indwelling spirit of grace. Entire Sanctification is the work of the Holy Spirit in cleansing the depths of the heart of the believer from self interest that is the source and mark of sin. It is received by faith in much the same way as the new birth is received. It opens the door to continuing growth in spiritual and moral conduct that comes through the ministry of the Indwelling Spirit throughout one's lifetime. A variety of images are employed to describe sanctification. One of these is "holiness of heart and life." This image suggests that the believer is enabled to live a life marked by purity of heart while enjoying the fullness and power of the Spirit.

Roman Catholics believe that the holy life results from a double calling. All Christians are called to follow Christ's teachings, but only a few are called to the higher standard of the "counsels of perfection." The effect of this is that Christian perfection becomes synonymous with the "religious life" including the vows of poverty, chastity, and obedience. A danger of this system is that the general Church community views serious discipleship as being part of the lifestyle only of those separated from the real world in the religious and monastic orders.

The early Protestant Reformers (especially Luther and Calvin) opposed the Roman Catholic belief of the "counsels of perfection" and viewed the mention of perfection as being inconsistent with a view of man's dependence upon grace. A person is "both justified and a sinner" until one arrives in heaven. In Luther's view, therefore, holiness is granted at only at death since holiness is required for entry into heaven (Heb. 12:14).

John Wesley taught that by the grace of God and through the work of the Spirit the believer can receive the perfection which Jesus urged upon His disciples (Matt. 5:48). This is not a perfection of performance but of love as the Spirit makes our passion for Christ the central and the all-determining factor in our lives. This does not in itself save us from making mistakes. [1] Nor does it remove all of our personality flaws. Nor does it take [2] away the possibility of sin. What it does do is unite our hearts to [3] God's heart. So the insistence upon our own way is gone and we are filled with a deep desire not to grieve our Lord who gave Himself for us. It produces the kind of undivided heart that will manifest itself in a holy life of love.

It is important for readers to remember that there are a number of very different understandings of exactly how and when sanctification occurs. Christians of all persuasions are united in their belief that sanctification must happen before one enters heaven's gates. Of course, sanctification is not an easily understood doctrine, but that does not release any of us from searching with heart and mind for God's will in regard to this matter.

Chapter Thirteen

The Hope of Glory

[I believe that] "He shall come to judge the quick and the dead,
[and I believe in] the resurrection of the body and the life everlasting"
(The Creed)

I. The Christian Hope

The Christian's hope for eternal life is built upon the foundation of the Old and New Testaments. This hope is grounded in the prophecies concerning the promised Messiah and the Second Coming of Christ. New Testament Christians waited, and present-day Christians are still waiting, for the return of Jesus Christ. Some Christians throughout the ages have become so involved in studying and watching for the return of the promised Messiah that they have neglected their daily Christian walk. The apostle Paul warned the early church of such things, lest they become lazy in daily activities and ignorant in faith (II Thess. 2:1-8; 3:6-10; II Pet. 3:3-9). Christians appropriately rejoice in the hope of eternal life with Christ while encouraging others to come to faith in Christ.

The Greek word *elpis* is used in the New Testament to express hope, expectation, and prospect. In Romans 8:24-25, Paul states, "For in this hope we were saved. Now hope that is

seen is not hope. For who hopes for what he sees? But I we hope
for what we do not see, we wait for it with patience." Christian
hope is ultimately grounded in the consistency of God. What
God has once begun, He will bring to complete fulfillment, for
He is an unchanging God whose purposes will be carried out.

II. The Second Advent

The Second Advent means the Second Coming of Christ
into this world. The First Advent occurred when God incar-
nated Himself in the birth of baby Jesus. Some acknowledge
the birth of Jesus as the First Advent, but view the Second
Advent as occurring in Acts 2:1-8, when the Holy Spirit was
poured out upon the gathered believers. A more traditional
view opposes this theory by referring to Revelation 1:7 and
Matthew 24:27-30. This view, then, is that the Lord's Second
Return will occur at an appointed time known only to God.
According to this position, the Christian has faith in the
goodness, power, and constancy of God, and believes that
history will end with Christ as the reigning King. The Greek
word that describes this coming in glory, or royal Presence, is
parousia. Another word that may be more familiar is *eschatology*. This term refers to the study of Last Things. The
Parousia will signal to humankind that God is ending the old
universe and beginning to reveal His new universe. God will
bind Satan with all his evil powers, thus allowing Christ to
reign supreme during the Millennial Kingdom.

III. The Millennial Kingdom

The concept of the millennial kingdom is a serious topic for
Christians seeking to understand eschatology. Christ and the
risen martyrs will rule this kingdom for one thousand years. The
stated time of "one thousand years" need not be interpreted in

a literal chronological manner. Hebrew thought can well be read and understood as highly symbolic. This symbolism does not reduce the Christian's degree of reverence for the authority of Scripture or place the length of the millennial kingdom in a category of being vague and hard to understand.

The expectation of the millennial kingdom illustrates the central truth that Christianity is not a hopeless religion. Rather, it is a faith that promises eternal life to all believers. The fitting climax to this promise is Christ's final and complete triumphant return to the world, which rejected and crucified Him as a common criminal. The whole world order is to be transformed under Christ so that the glory of God may be fully revealed.

In discussions of the Second Advent and the millennial kingdom, the leader of the forces of evil is often called the Antichrist. He should not be confused with the real person of Satan, the leader of evil in the world since the fall of Adam and Eve. Individuals desiring to establish the identity of the Antichrist have done much research and study. It is the conviction of the writers of this book that our study should center on the person of Jesus Christ. This approach will go far to avoid being tricked by the Antichrist.

The ideal society is not built by the power of man alone. It is the work of the mighty power of God as it works within His creatures. The teaching of the millennial kingdom symbolizes this. Of course it should be born in mind that not all evangelical Christians employ millennial terminology.

IV. Human Destiny

Eternal life is an everlasting fellowship with God. This does not mean simply survival after death or an existence of endless duration. Eternal life is a quality of life that we know as our present gift because we are joined to God by faith in Christ. It is not something we hope to possess only after death. As Christians we experience a life of inner joy because we have faith in the goodness of God. This joy is a gift of grace given by God to those who are united with Him through faith in Christ. Believers cannot earn eternal life just as they cannot earn salvation.

The sovereign God, who created humankind and redeemed them in Christ, has freely committed Himself to giving eternal life to His children. It would be inconsistent with the character of God, revealed in Christ, to raise the hope of fellowship with Him and then to disappoint this hope by destroying humankind at death.

Immortality and *resurrection* are two closely related terms. *Immortality* means that the spiritual dimension of man cannot be destroyed. The spirit of a person continues after the death and decay of the material body. *Resurrection* may be defined in terms of spirit, body, or both. It is the raising of the Christian's spirit or soul immediately after death; it is also the bodily resurrection of all the human dead to appear before the final judgment.

Our faith affirms that the souls of departed Christians are alive to serve God more fully and to live in communion with Him. Or perhaps more widely held is the idea that Christians living or dead enjoy a fellowship due to the spiritual union with each other and with Jesus Christ. This is called the "communion of saints." This belief in immortality holds that the departed saints are in fellowship with God.

The biblical teaching of the resurrection of believers argues that the person who is alive at the day of God's triumph will be complete in every aspect. The glorified body of the resurrected believer will be like that of the resurrected body of Christ. This body is flawless in all areas, spiritually, physically, and mentally. Just as Christ's resurrected body is glorified, so will be the believer's body.

V. Divine Judgment

The Bible is consistent in its teaching that judgment is both present and future. When the believer cooperates with the Holy Spirit, one opens the door to a more vital relationship with God. In contrast, continual refusal to cooperate with the Holy Spirit results in a hardening of the heart that leads to spiritual death.

Divine judgment is God's predictable response to sin. In the New Testament, God's response to sin is termed the wrath of God; however, this is not a vindictive response on God's part. It is a proper response on the part of God to the state of moral corruption that is the result of one's idolatry, self-centeredness, and rebellious pride. (see Rom. 1:18-32).

The last judgment differs from the present process of judgment in two important ways. The present judgment is a secret judgment, known only to God. The last judgment is an open judgment, in which all people will be called to account fully for their actions, good and bad. The present judgment is a conditional judgment that encourages the sinner to find mercy through repentance. The last judgment is final and seals the fate of all people. The final judgment will involve all Christians whose mediator is Christ. This means that Christians who do not keep themselves in a daily devotional and love relationship with Christ may fall away and risk losing their salvation.

The concepts of heaven and hell are directly related to the final judgment. The scriptures have divided the judgment into two distinct groups, the lost and the saved. From the perspective of this understanding, lost and unrepentant sinners are cast into hell, whereas the saved, followers of Christ, are resurrected into heaven. Both placements are final and eternal.

Hell is described in the Bible as a lake of fire. The discussion as to whether hell is a place or merely a spiritual state of being is and will continue to be an unanswerable question. The reasoning behind the idea of hell as a spiritual state of being is the thought that when God withdraws His Holy Spirit and Christian disciples from the earth there will be no source of good to counteract the evil of this world.

Ultimately, the writers of this book are united in their belief that the Bible is not to be used as a sourcebook for speculation about the end times. Rather, it is a revelation of Truth as well as a spiritual, ethical, and devotional guide, addressed to actual situations of daily living. The clear teaching of the Bible in light of this is that the unrepentant sinner will receive eternal punishment; the repentant believer will be eternally blessed. The unified longing of the Christian hope, then, is for the final blessedness of being glorified in order to see God face to face, and forever to join in worshiping Him. "Blessed are the pure in heart, for they shall see God" (Matt. 5:8).